# ME & MY BALLPOINT PEN

## DRAWING SKILLS AND ABSTRACT DRILLS FOR ARTISTIC EXCELLENCE

JENNIFER MULLIN

DAVID & CHARLES
—PUBLISHING—

www.davidandcharles.com

# CONTENTS

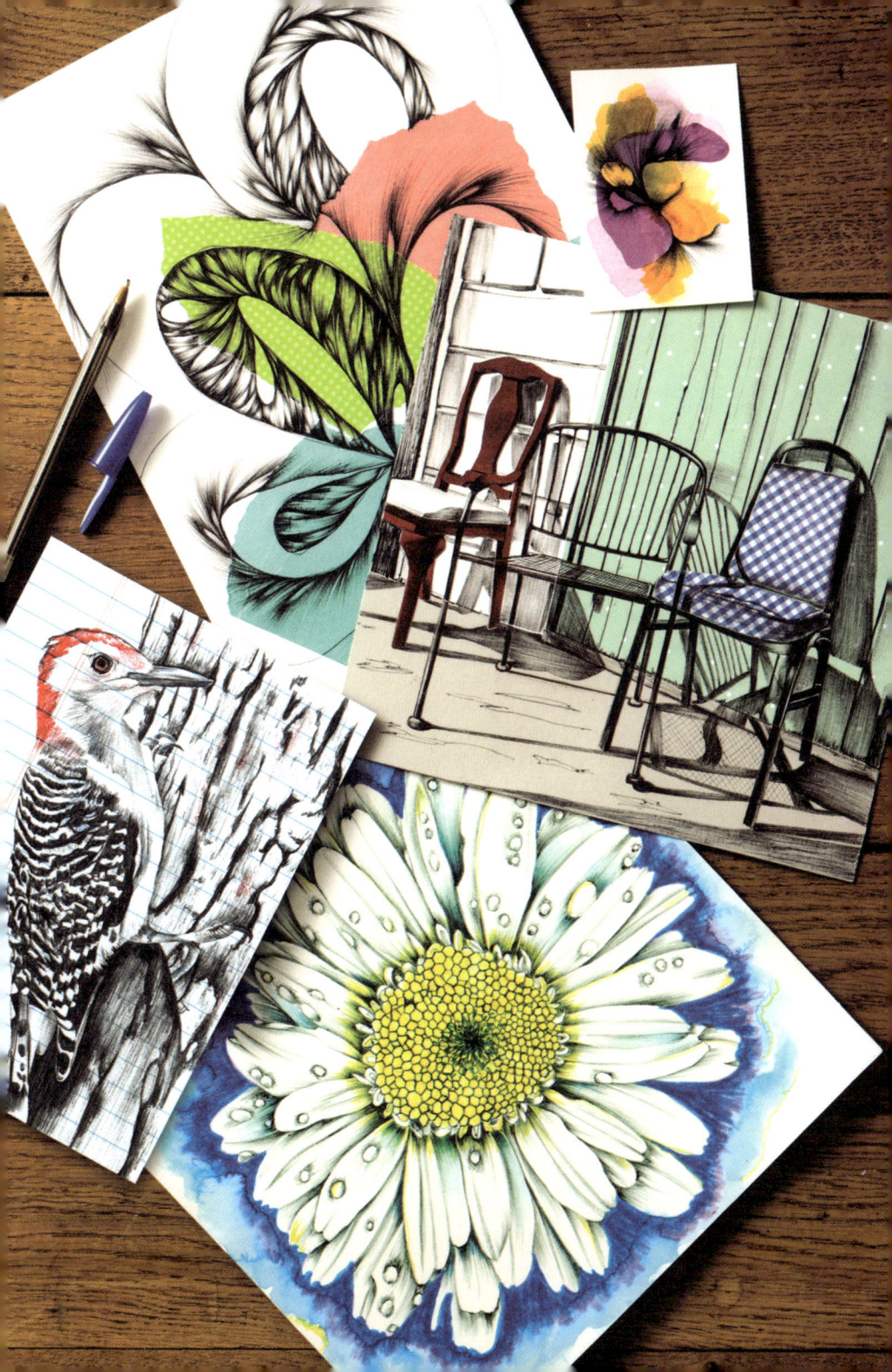

# INTRODUCTION

The ubiquitous ballpoint pen is a fantastic drawing tool. It's inexpensive, ultra portable, and is available in a wide range of colors. With a pen, I can draw anywhere, any time (often on my couch with a cat nearby and the TV on in the background).

I really got hooked on drawing with ballpoints during my time as an art teacher. While I was sitting in meetings, I'd often draw as I listened. After years of filling sketchbooks, I developed a series of marks and techniques that I came back to over and over again. With lots of time and space for experimentation and play, I developed a signature style all of my own.

Weirdly, the "finished work" I was making and selling at the time had nothing to do with my pen sketches. I was deep into mixed media collage and watercolor, with some technical pen work thrown in. Eventually, my pen work and my mixed media work intertwined. I started using pen to shade in my illustrations, and over time, pen crept into every piece I made.

For years, I drew chairs, birds, florals, and abstracts, all with a black pen, helping me to master the art of shading with a pen. Finally, I began to feel limited by only using black ink, and started experimenting with pens of every color, especially in my abstract work and never looked back.

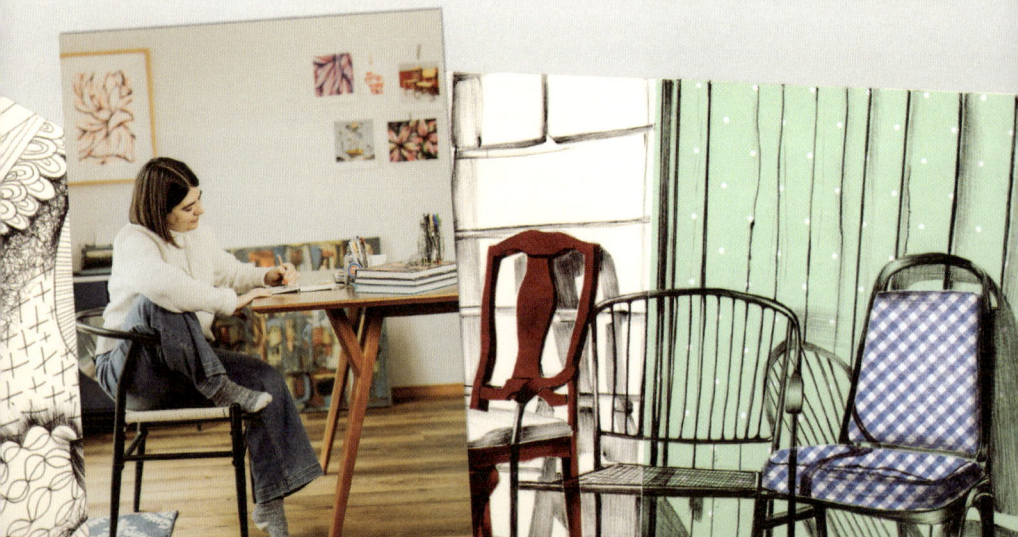

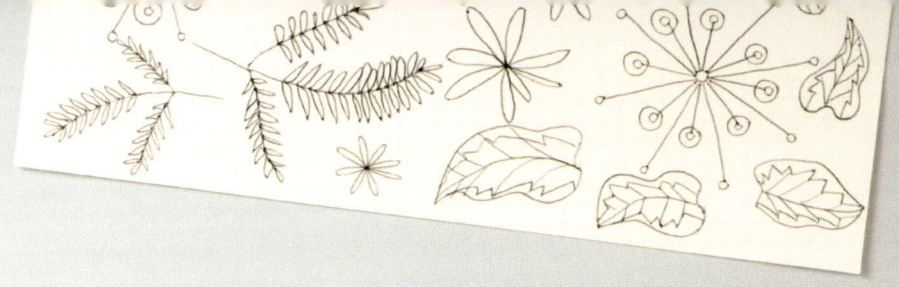

Around this time, my multicolor abstract pen sketches went viral on Pinterest. People were enamored with my work and I received hundreds of requests for instruction. Enter the "Jen + Ink" ballpoint drawing courses, where I teach my abstract pen drawing techniques. I certainly hit a nerve with these, as they've been taken by thousands around the world.

For almost a decade now, ballpoint pens have been my primary drawing tool. I'm continually inspired and challenged by the humble pen and I foresee many more years of creative exploration with a pen in hand.

In this book, you will learn how to render both realistically and abstractly with a ballpoint pen. I'll share all of my ballpoint drawing secrets that I've picked up over the years and show you how to use the humble ballpoint to create expressive, detailed art.

Ballpoint drawing is a slow, meditative process. I can spend hours over several days on one sketchbook spread, so don't feel like you must complete the exercises in this book in one sitting. Take your time and enjoy the process.

My hope is that this book inspires you to explore ballpoint, learn the basics, and then make them your own. I've included detailed step-by-step instructions to get you going, as well as some more open-ended projects that you could take in any direction you please.

Jennifer

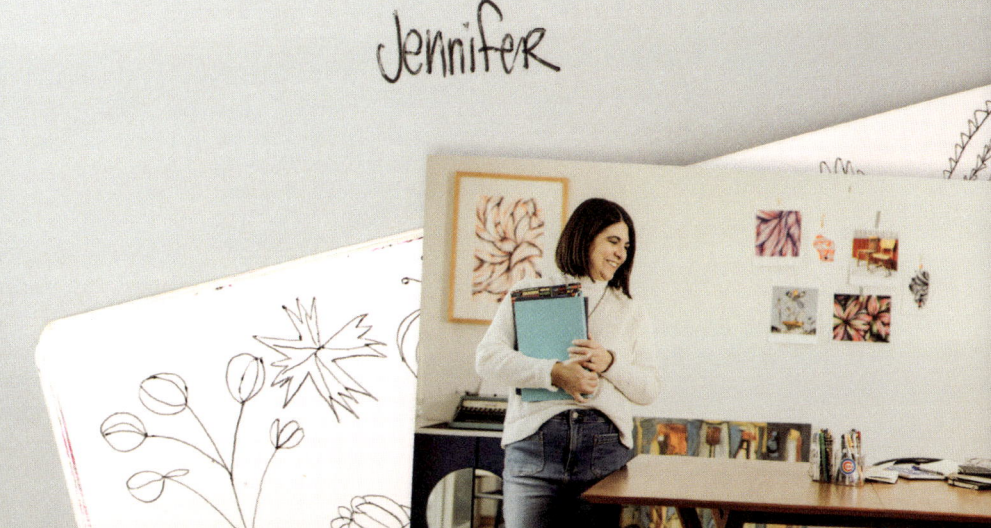

# A SHORT HISTORY OF THE BALLPOINT

Everyone knows what a ballpoint pen is and no doubt have several around the home. However, most people don't know about the history of the pen and how it became a universal tool.

## Origins

Ballpoints were an upgrade on the fountain pen, which had a tendency to leak and smear. They were scratchy and it was difficult to control the flow of ink. On top of that, they were expensive and out of reach for most people.

The first version of a ballpoint came in 1888 from American leather tanner John J Loud, who was looking for a practical way to mark on leather. By replacing the nib of the pen with a ball bearing, the ink would, in theory, spread more evenly. Compared to modern ballpoints, the ball bearing was enormous. It worked well on leather but was too big and too rough for paper, so it never sold, and eventually the patent lapsed.

For the next 40 years, many other attempts were made to perfect the ballpoint technology for writing on paper, but with limited success. As these early ballpoints relied on gravity to feed the ink, they didn't work at all angles. Additionally, the ball bearings often leaked and the water-based inks would seep into the fibers of the paper and spread.

## The Birome

In the 1930s, Hungarian-Argentinian newspaper man, László Bíró set out to make a pen that didn't smudge when writing. He enlisted the help of his chemist brother, György, and together they created a quick-drying, highly viscous ink. The oil-based ink formulation sat on top of the paper and kept the ball constantly covered in ink. A slight redesign of the pen allowed for ink to be pulled onto the ball without gravity and when not in use, the ball basically plugged the ink reservoir, preventing leaks.

This ballpoint worked from every angle and allowed for consistent, precise ink flow on paper. Bíró patented and started selling his design as the "Birome" but they never really took off outside of South America. At $190 each in today's money, they were cost prohibitive and the ballpoint pen remained a luxury item. Despite the lack of financial success with his invention, his name became synonymous with the pen, and in many countries ballpoints are still referred to as biros.

While visiting Buenos Aires, American businessman Milton Reynolds came across the Birome pen and was intrigued. Making enough changes to sidestep Bíró's patent, the Reynolds Rocket was introduced in 1945 and sold thousands in the first week. A huge selling point was its ability to write for two years without having to be refilled. But like the Birome, it was on the expensive side and because it was gravity fed, it still had a tendency to leak.

## The Bic Cristal

The ballpoint pen was truly perfected in 1950 by French manufacturer Marcel Bich when he purchased the ballpoint patent from Bíró. By redesigning the ball bearing for mass production and using extruded plastic for the body of the pen, Bich significantly lowered the price point of the ballpoint. The Bic Cristal ballpoint pen was born and quickly spread around the world. More than 100 billion Bic Cristals have been sold and the design is so good that it's barely changed since it was introduced in 1950. This simple but ingenious bit of technology democratized writing and in turn, literacy rates soared.

## A drawing tool

Artists quickly adopted the ballpoint as a drawing tool and has been used over the years by many well-known artists including Alberto Giacometti, Andy Warhol, John Cage, Cy Twombly, and Louise Bourgeois. Contemporary artists like myself continue to create art with ballpoint pens, and the manner in which they are used is about as wide-ranging as the pen itself.

Today, there are many iterations of the ballpoint pen available, and they all rely on the technology of Bich's design. You'd be hard-pressed to find a home, school, or office anywhere without at least one ballpoint pen inside.

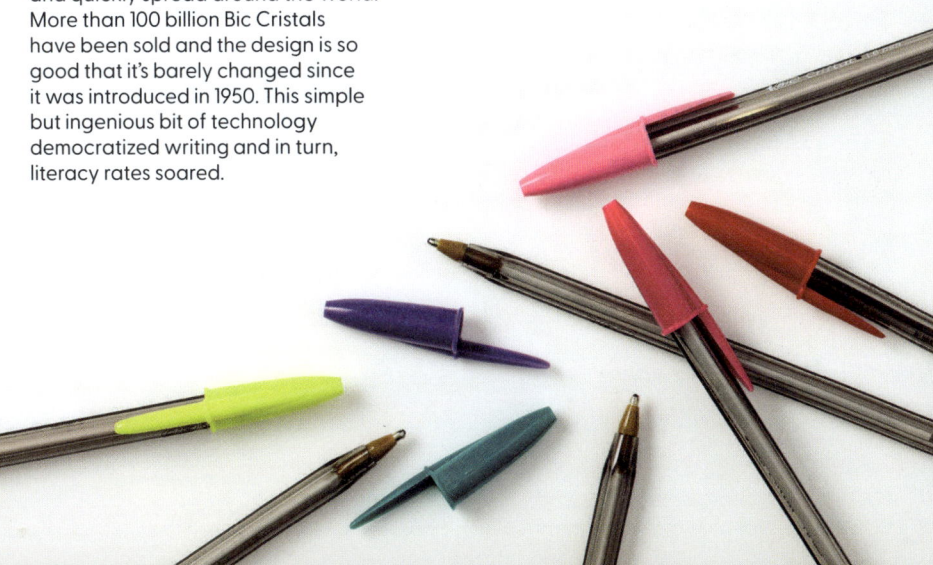

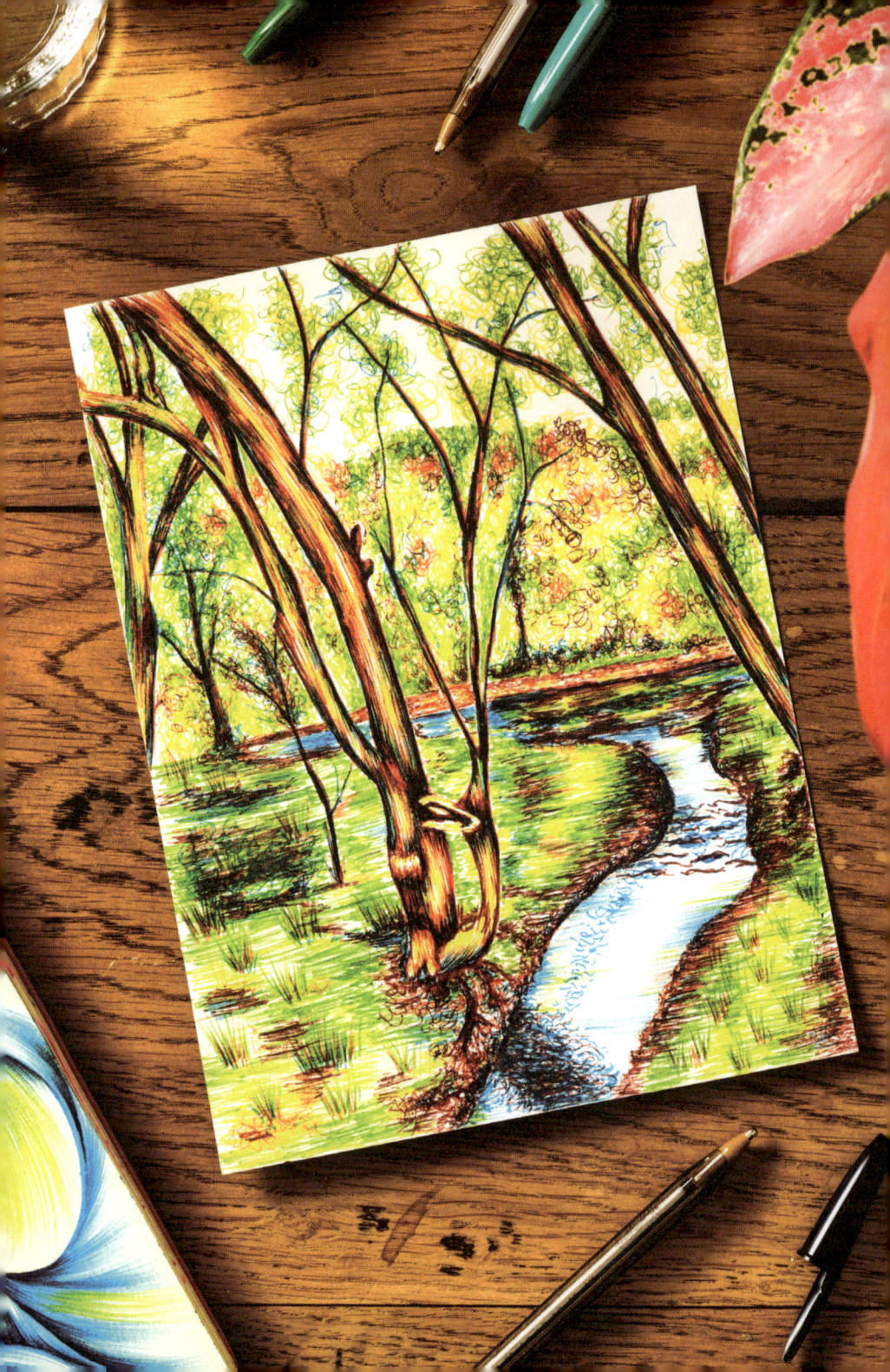

# SET YOURSELF UP FOR SUCCESS

I truly believe that drawing is for everyone, and I hope that what you find in this book will inspire you to create. To get the most out of this book and your creative journey, here's a bit of practical advice.

## 1. Work at your own pace

It may take some time to get the hang of drawing with a ballpoint. Give yourself grace and don't be discouraged if you don't get it right away. The more you practice, the more intuitive and easy it will become.

## 2. Enjoy the process

Relax and allow yourself to create without judgment or concern for the outcome. Draw because you want to. Draw because it brings you joy.

## 3. Take breaks

Drawing with a ballpoint can be quite time-consuming and a little tedious. Take a step away from your work every once in a while to rest. You'll come back with fresh eyes and more confidence, and will probably enjoy yourself a whole lot more.

## 4. Embrace imperfections

Mistakes are bound to happen. Please don't let them derail you. Imperfections give your work character and personality. If you can't live with them, there is usually a way to fix or hide them. It's also perfectly acceptable to start anew if that feels right.

## 5. Make it your own

This book is intended to be a jumping-off point for your own artistic journey. In the beginning, you may just be copying my work, but as you get more comfortable working with ballpoints, I hope that you develop your own marks, techniques, and compositions that are uniquely yours. If your drawings look nothing like mine, consider that a success!

# TOOLS AND MATERIALS

There's a good chance you have what you need to make a ballpoint drawing at home already: a pen and some smooth paper. Here are some more suggestions to get you started.

## Ballpoint pens

Every brand of pen has a slightly different point, ink formulation, and color. I suggest experimenting with as many different brands as you can to find what works best for you. Use a pen that feels good and is most comfortable in your hand.

## Pen widths

Pens with wider points lend themselves to even shading, and are usually around 1.3mm or more. Pens with fine points are best for detail and sharp edges. Look for points that are 0.8mm or smaller.

## Refillable pens

I've become partial to refillable ballpoint pens. I appreciate that I'm using less plastic and I like the weight of the metal pen in my hand. A build up of ink doesn't occur so readily with refillable pens, so it's less likely for a blob of ink to end up where you don't want it (I discuss this in greater detail later in the book). One drawback is the color range. There are only a handful of colors available in refillable cartridge form.

## Paper

I find it easiest to draw with pens on smooth paper. The smoother the paper, the easier it will be to achieve even shading. If you're just starting out, consider buying a ream of cheap, white copy paper. That way, you won't feel guilty if you blow through a ton of it when you're learning and practicing your technique.

## Scratch paper

I suggest keeping some scrap paper on hand for cleaning ink off pens and to place under your drawing hand to prevent the transfer of ink. It can be whatever you have, including bits of paper you have already used.

## Sketchbooks

I do most of my pen drawing in sketchbooks. Again, look for the smoothest paper you can find. I gravitate towards sketchbooks that lie flat with thick paper pages (150gsm or higher).

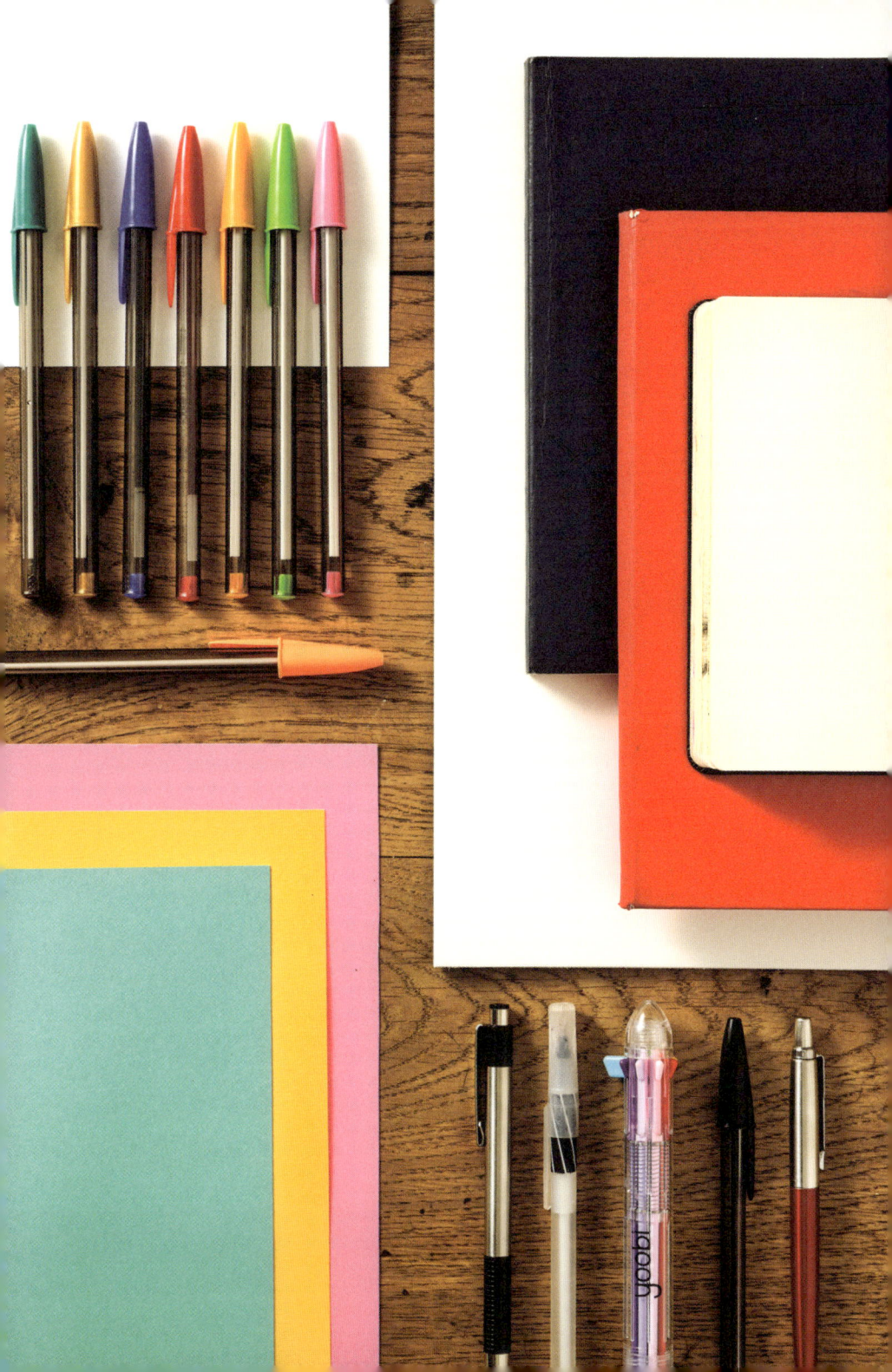

## Bristol board

Smooth Bristol board is ideal for pen drawing. This substantial paper has a super-smooth surface that makes it easy to work on. There are many different finishes of Bristol board available, so be sure to look for the smooth version. Anything with a texture will be more difficult to work on.

## Marker paper

Marker paper also makes a good surface for pens. Similar to Bristol board, it's smooth and is designed to prevent ink bleeding through.

## Wet media

If you're looking to incorporate some wet media into your pen sketches, I'd recommend hot press watercolor paper or mixed media paper. It's smooth enough for pens, but will stand up to watercolor or fluid inks.

## Other supplies

A pencil (HB or lighter), an eraser, a ruler, glue stick, and scissors will all come in handy. A cutting mat will also be useful for collage work. It protects your work surface and if you get a self-healing one, it will remain flat. Spare cardboard is a good alternative.

## Preservation materials

There is one downfall to my beloved pen: the ink is very susceptible to fading. Unfortunately, I learned this the hard way after many of my older pieces discolored over time. Here are some things you can do and use to prevent fading.

- Draw with acid-free, archival quality ink on archival paper. There are archival ink pens on the market, most of them are refillable. Look for a pen with an oil-based ink.

- Most disposable pens have a dye-based ink that will degrade quite rapidly. In general, blue and black are more lightfast than other colors.

- Applying a layer of UV spray varnish provides a minimal layer of protection. I've still noticed fading on pieces that I've sprayed, especially if they are hung in direct light.

- Frame your finished drawings behind UV resistant glass or acrylic. Though pricey, museum-quality glass can block 99 percent of UV rays.

- Hang work away from direct sunlight. My favorite pen drawing is displayed at the base of the staircase in my home, where it receives no direct sunlight.

- Scan or photograph your original drawing and have a print made to put on display.

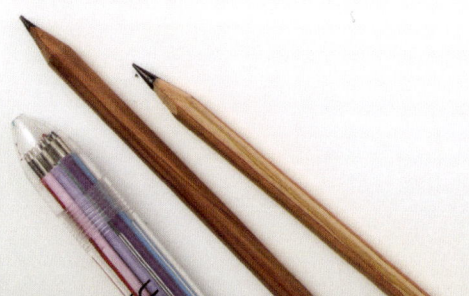

## Terminology

### Substrate
In art work, this refers to any surface that you can draw or paint on, such as paper, canvas, or Bristol board.

### Format
When I talk about format, I'm referring to the shape and/or size of the paper.

### Notes
I use this term to mean a rough draft or an outline, where you just plan out what will happen next in the drawing.

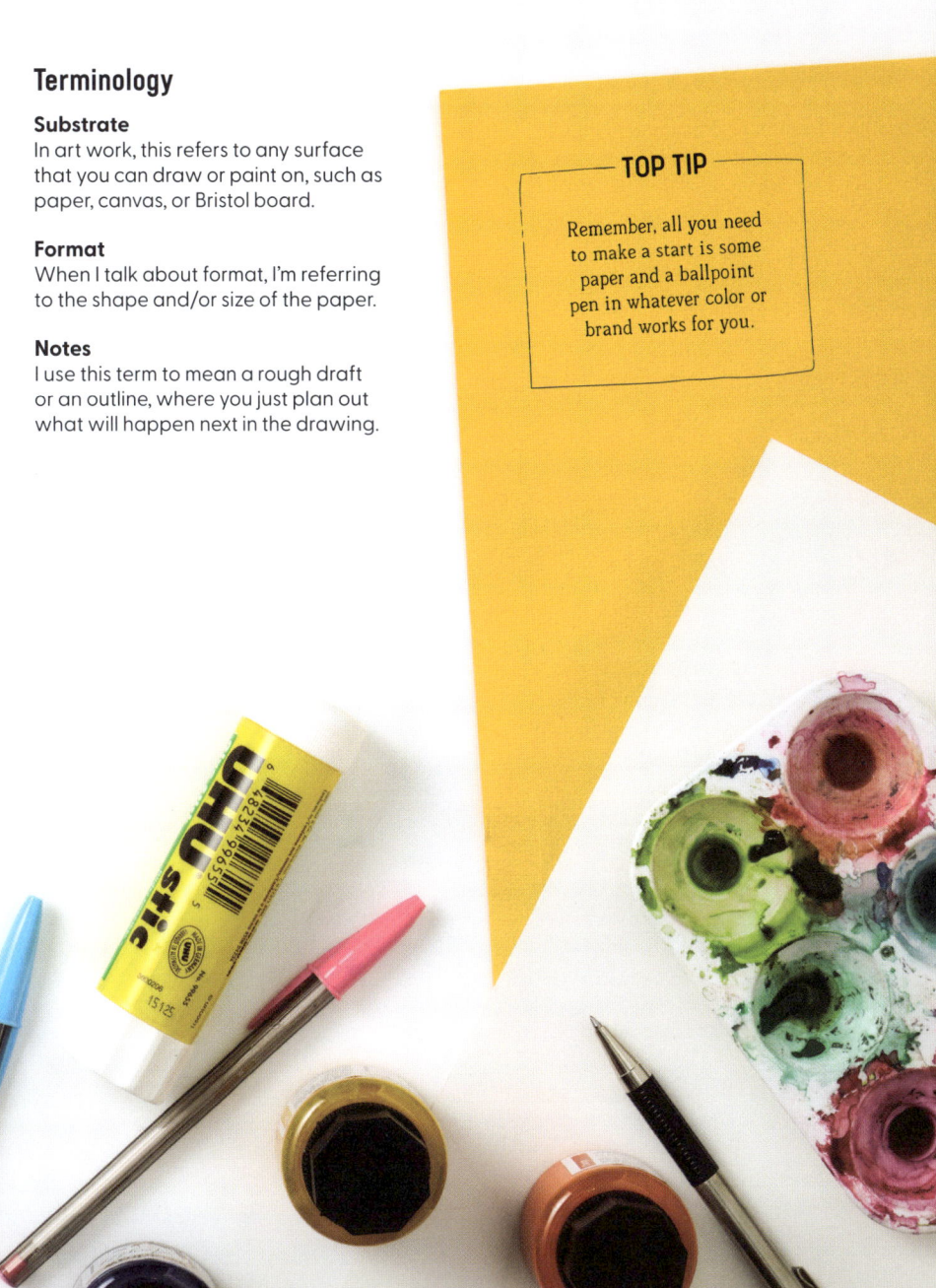

### TOP TIP

Remember, all you need to make a start is some paper and a ballpoint pen in whatever color or brand works for you.

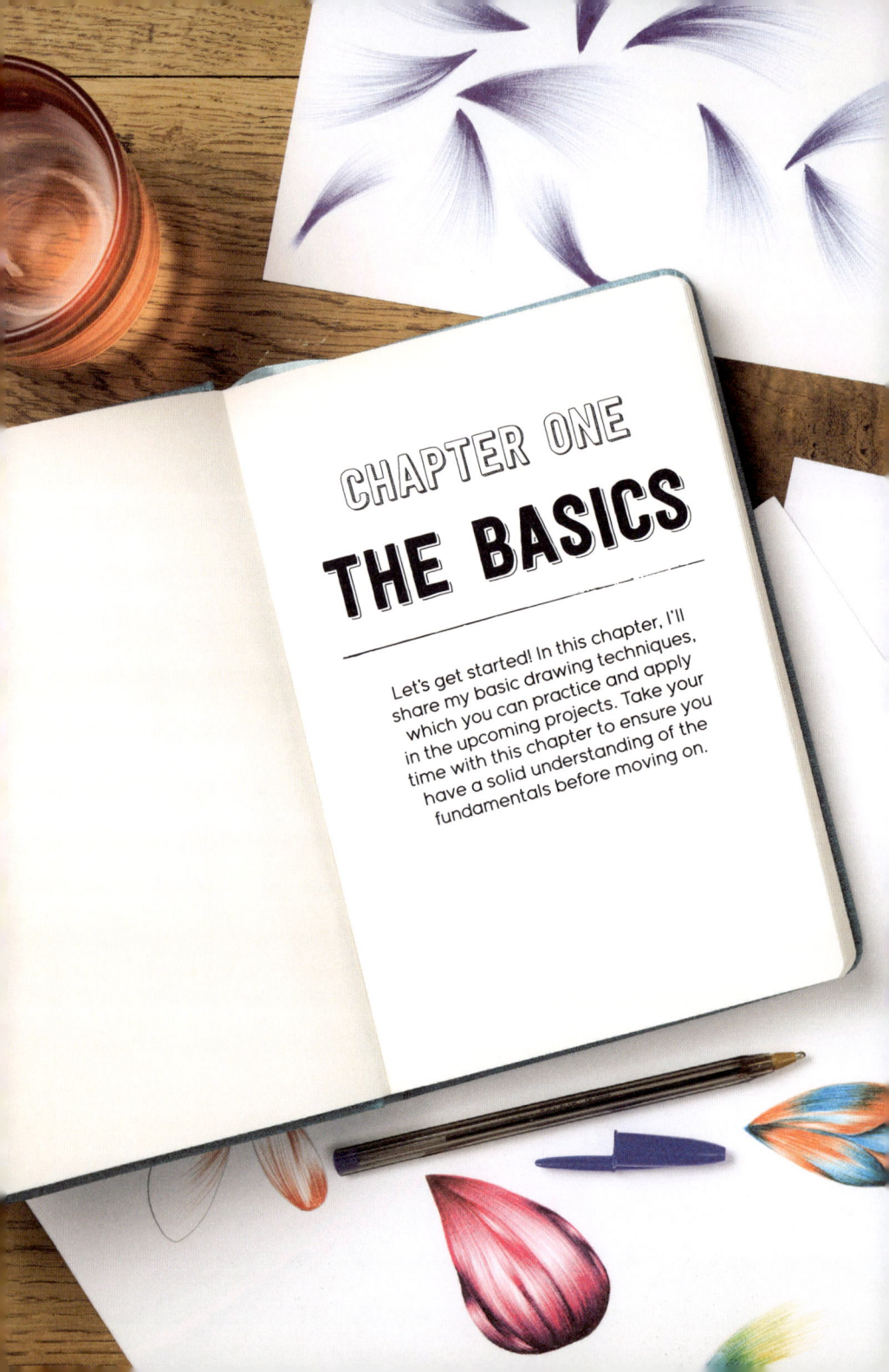

# CHAPTER ONE

# THE BASICS

Let's get started! In this chapter, I'll share my basic drawing techniques, which you can practice and apply in the upcoming projects. Take your time with this chapter to ensure you have a solid understanding of the fundamentals before moving on.

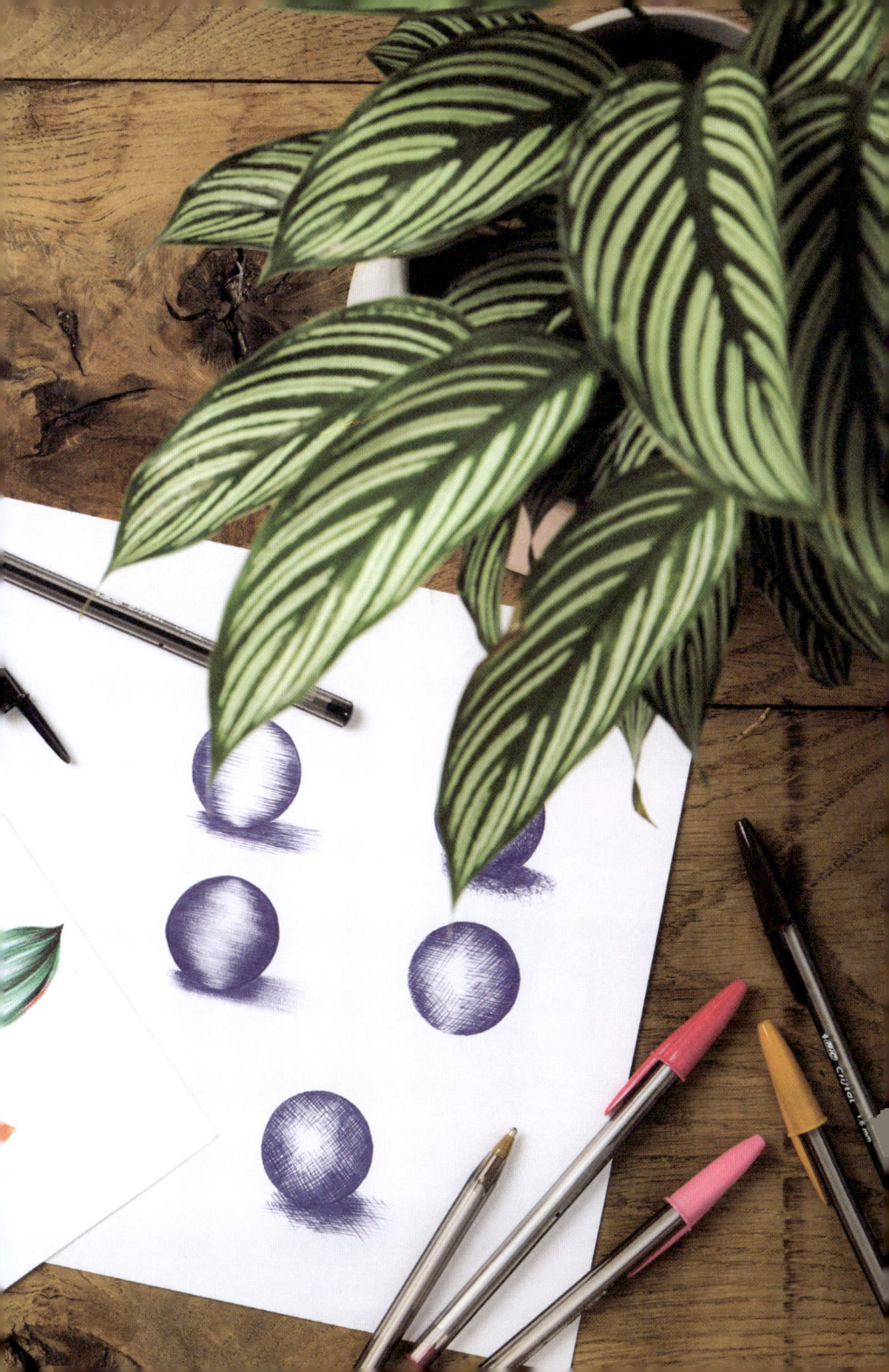

# VALUE

The term value refers to the degree of lightness or darkness in your drawing. Not only does value add interest to your work, but it also creates a sense of depth and dimension.

Since we see and understand objects because of how dark or light they are, value is an incredibly important element of art. You can achieve a full range of dark, medium, and light values with a ballpoint, as it's all about the pressure you use.

Dark values are quite easy to achieve with a pen. The more pressure you exert on the pen, the darker the marks will be. Instead of pressing really hard on the paper, I tend to build up strokes slowly. There's no erasing with ballpoint, so I'd rather add them mindfully.

I've always found it more difficult to create light values. It takes some practice to train your hand to apply the light pressure needed to establish even, light values. The lightest value in a pen drawing is the white of the paper, so it's important to retain some white space to achieve a full range of values.

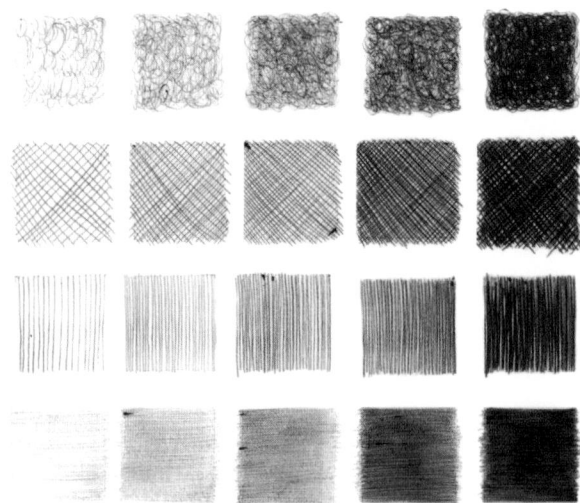

# CONTRAST

Contrast is another important concept. It can take many forms, but most simply, contrast is differences in art elements. Differences in values, colors, and textures create contrast, making them stand out in a work of art.

Consider the difference, or contrast, between dark and light values, or between organic shapes and geometric shapes.

Contrast creates visual interest and helps the viewer interpret the drawing. Without a full range of value, which helps achieve contrast, pen drawings can appear flat and uninteresting.

Other examples of contrast might include:

- Color: red and green
- Texture: smooth and rough
- Lines: wavy/curved and straight
- Shapes: organic and geometric.

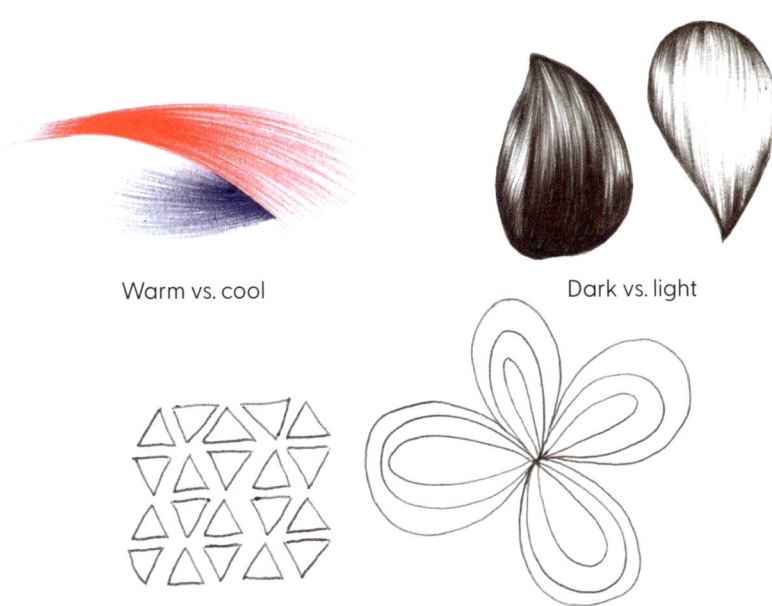

Warm vs. cool

Dark vs. light

Geometric vs. organic

# MY SHADING TECHNIQUE

I enjoy using ballpoints to create smooth, even values, so that the individual strokes of the pen are obscured. There's a bit of a learning curve to shading in this manner, but once you get the hang of it, I hope you find it as relaxing as I do.

Pens with traditional ink colors (blue, black, red, green) tend to flow more evenly, so I suggest starting with these colors. Keep some scratch paper nearby so you can clean off the build-up of ink that collects on the point of the pen. I often put another piece of paper underneath my drawing hand so that I don't smudge the ink that I've already laid down on the paper.

My technique is all about "the touch." Using a light grip on the pen, gently brush the point across the paper, making light, fluid strokes. The lighter the touch, the more even a value you'll be able to achieve.

As I'm left-handed, I prefer to work with downward strokes. Some of my right-handed students report that it feels more comfortable to make upward strokes. Whatever feels natural to you is what you should do. There are no hard and fast rules to this.

Try working through this shading exercise to build up your knowledge and your confidence.

## Step one

To develop that "touch," work on making patches of even values with a wide-point pen on smooth paper (the smoother the paper, the better). The goal is to make the patches look like one mass of value instead of individual strokes of the pen.

Don't worry about the value of the marks to begin with, just concentrate on your technique. You probably won't be able to achieve an even, smooth value in one layer. Oftentimes, I have to work back over areas to fill in and even out the value, so most of your initial patches will probably be in the medium value range.

## Step two

Continue to focus on the technique. If it gets tedious to work in just one color, use two or three. This is also a good way of experimenting with different brands of pen to see which one you like best. Try to fill up a whole page, with the goal of creating smooth, even values. The more you practice, the more natural and intuitive the technique will become.

## Step three

If you're struggling to create even values, consider working in multiple directions, like cross-hatching. After you lay down one layer, turn your paper 90 degrees and add another layer. This helps to further obscure the individual pen strokes.

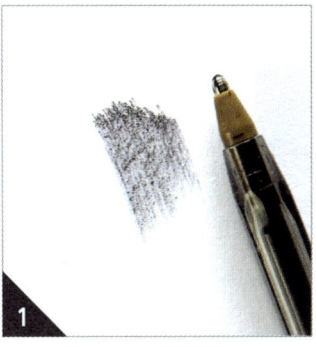

## Step four

As you get more comfortable with the technique, experiment with going darker and lighter. The darker you want to go, the more layers of pen you'll add with a bit more pressure. Try to avoid pressing too hard, as you might impress lines into the paper. Instead, gradually work your way to a dark value.

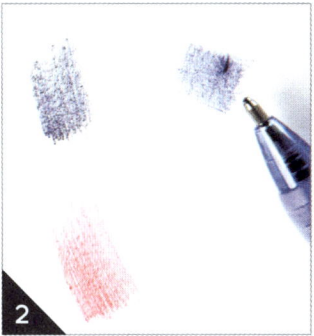

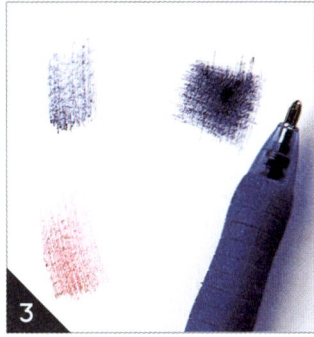

### TOP TIP

Pay attention to the pen as you work, removing any ink buildup so it doesn't end up on your drawing. If you do get a rogue spot of dark ink, don't panic. Simply go darker around it to blend it away.

# OTHER SHADING TECHNIQUES

Though I'll mainly focus on my smooth shading technique in this book, I want to share some additional ways to add value with a pen. In these techniques, the individual strokes of the pen are more visible.

## Hatching

Hatching is a quick way of shading with straight lines, all in the same direction. Value and dimension is achieved by building up a collection of lines in various concentrations. Many artists hatch with short, straight lines in a uniform value, following the contour of the form, but feel free to work in a way that's most comfortable and effective for you. I find it's easiest to hatch with a fine- or medium-point pen.

## Cross-hatching

As the name suggests, cross-hatching involves drawing lines in two or more directions in a cross-like pattern. To create the most dimension in your drawing, work diagonally away from the edges of the forms. Cross-hatching is great for architectural drawing and adding value to clothing. I'd suggest a fine- or medium-point pen for this technique.

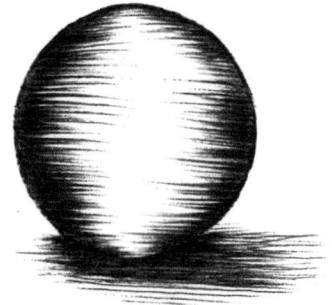
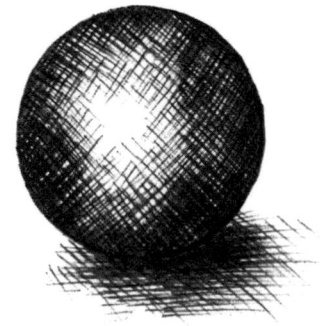

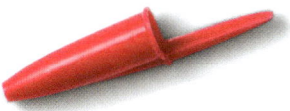

## Scribbling

Yes, you can scribble! This technique is especially effective when drawing landscapes and even animals. There is no right or wrong way to scribble. Just like every other shading technique, it's all about the "touch." Use a light touch to achieve light values. Gradually build up marks, pressing harder with each successive layer to create darks. I like to scribble with a medium- or wide-point pen.

## TOP TIP

As I am left-handed, I start on the right edge of an image, so that I don't drag my hand through the ink as I work. If you're right handed, you may want to start on the left side.

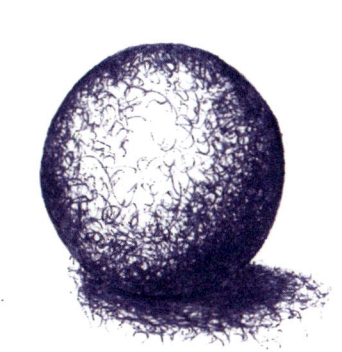

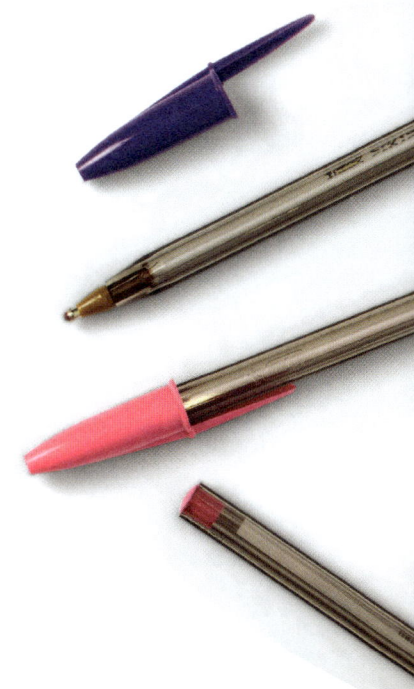

# TRANSITIONS

Once you've gotten the hang of shading evenly with a pen, try creating a transition. Also known as a gradient, it's a gradual change in value from light to dark. Transitions are used to create the illusion of depth and roundness in a two-dimensional drawing. The more gradual the transition, the more realistic the sense of space you can achieve.

Have patience with yourself as you learn this technique, as there is a learning curve and it can be time-consuming. Once you get the hang of it, transitions will raise the level of sophistication in your work.

Follow the steps in this exercise to practice creating transitions.

## TOP TIP

Use scratch paper to blot ink and to put under your drawing hand to avoid transferring any ink from your hand to the drawing.

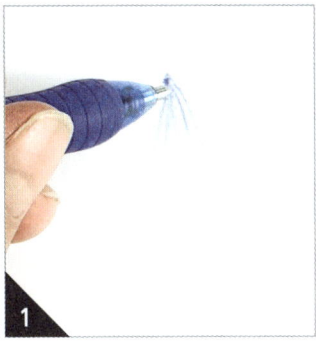

## Step one

Using a wide-point pen in a traditional color (blue, black, red, or green) on some smooth paper, add your first marks using a light touch. Build up an area of overall light shading. I tend to create a curved triangular shape.

## Step two

Go as dark as you can at the top point of the shaded area, but avoid pressing too hard so as not to emboss your paper. Continue building with light layers until there is a gradual change from dark to light. The goal is to make the value change seamless, with the dark values slowly fading into a medium and eventually a light value.

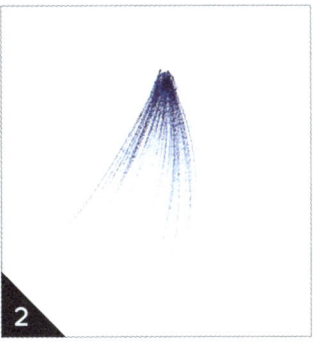

## Step three

Try not to end the transition in a straight line. Instead, vary the ending points of your strokes. This creates interest and makes the transition appear even more gradual. Practice creating gradual transitions by filling the page with them. Use one color or multiple colors, and don't worry about what the finished page looks like. It's just practice! The more you draw in this manner, the more natural it will become.

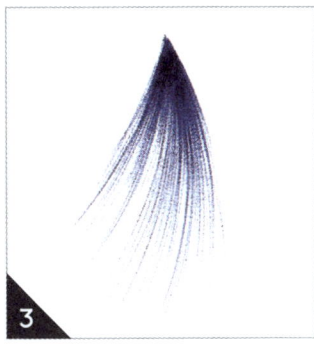

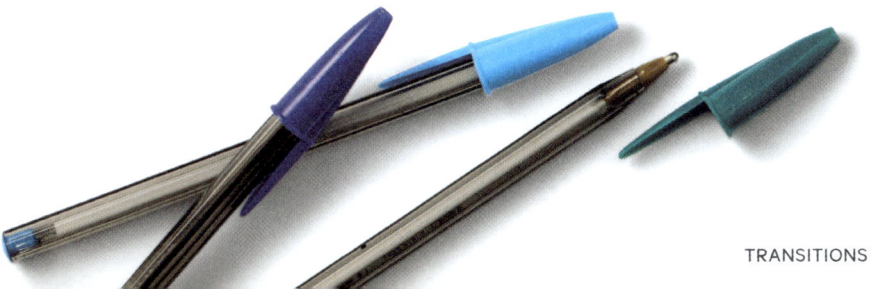

# COMPOSITION

Composition is the way that different elements are arranged in a work of art and it's an important skill for any artist. While there is not one definitive set of rules that all artists follow, there are some basic principles that can be applied to most artworks. Understanding and applying those principles adds sophistication and elegance to your art.

## Important components for a strong composition

**Repetition:** Repeating lines, shapes, and colors creates unity within a composition.

**Variety:** To create interest in your artwork, vary the size, shape, line, texture, and any other element in your composition. Using the same technique over and over will bore the viewer. Variety is the spice of life, after all.

**Negative and positive space:** Positive space can be described as the main forms in a composition. Negative space is the area surrounding the main form(s). In a good composition, both the negative and positive space should be interesting and balanced, but the negative space should not take away from the main forms.

**Contrast:** Differences in values, colors, textures, and other art elements make them stand out in a work of art and create visual interest (see Contrast earlier in this chapter).

**Overlapping:** In an interesting work of art, design elements overlap one another to create unity. Your eye follows the path that is created by the overlapping elements.

**Cropping:** Here, the artist leaves something to the imagination by drawing objects that go off the edge of the page. It makes the viewer wonder what is missing and creates visual interest.

**Focal point or center of interest:** Visually, this is the most important part of your artwork and where your eye is drawn to in the composition. Best placement of your center of interest is slightly off-center. Unless your design is symmetrical, a focal point should not be in the center of the format. The center of interest usually stands out from the rest of the composition.

Repetition  Negative space  Positive space

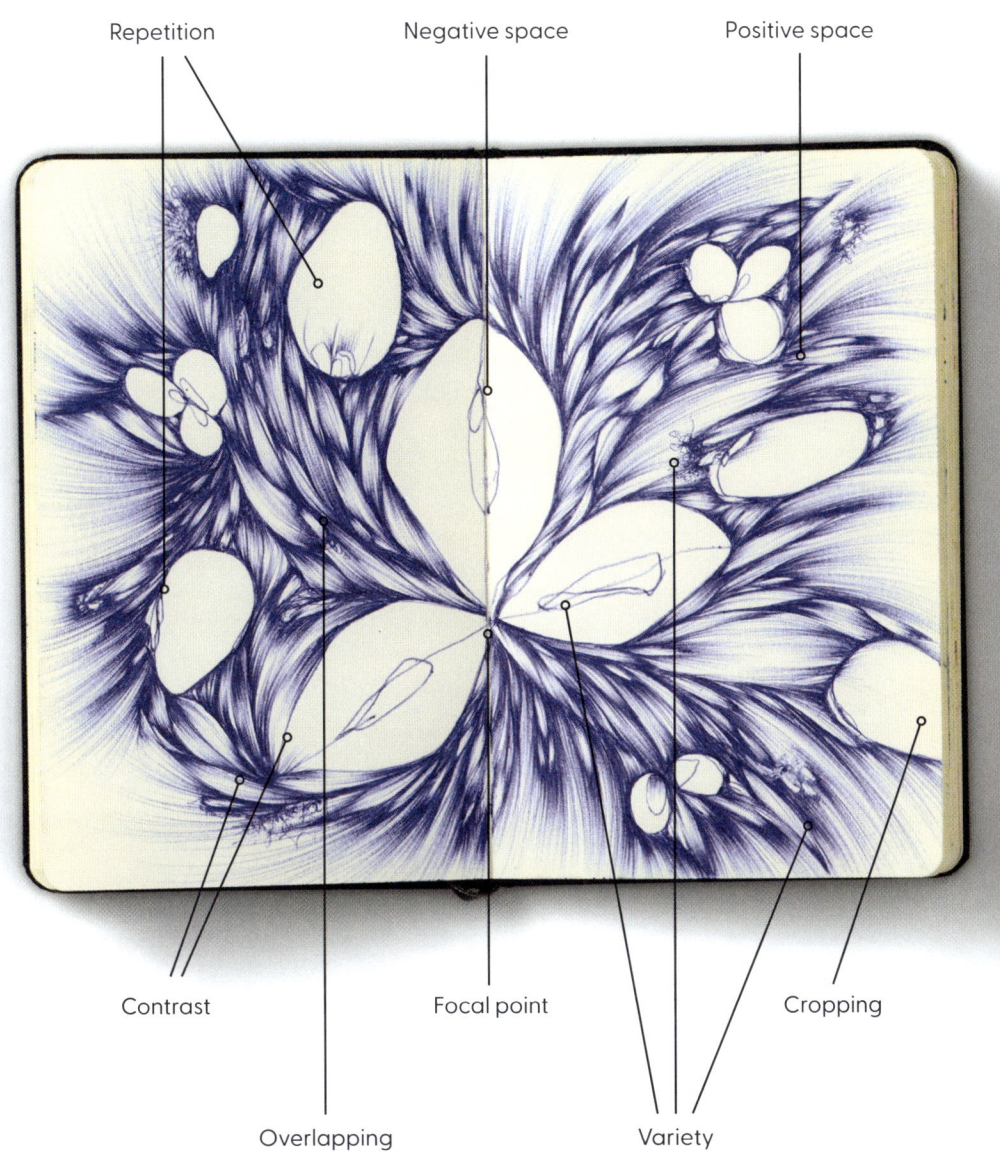

Contrast  Focal point  Cropping

Overlapping  Variety

If you're wondering if you've created a pleasing composition, ask yourself the following questions:

- Have you used the whole format?
- Do shapes run off three or more edges of the format?
- Do you make good use of your negative space? Is there variety in the amount of space between shapes?
- Have you avoided placing shapes directly into the composition from the corners or in the middle of the format?
- Have you avoided placing shapes in long lines that appear to divide the format into two?
- Do your shapes end at different levels?

- Is there a balanced, stable feeling?
- Is there variety in size, shape, value, and amount of detail?
- Is there a shape that is repeated, resulting in greater unity?
- Is there a focal point or center of interest that catches your eye?
- Do you have good eye flow and movement throughout the whole composition?
- Have you overlapped elements to show spatial depth and create unity?

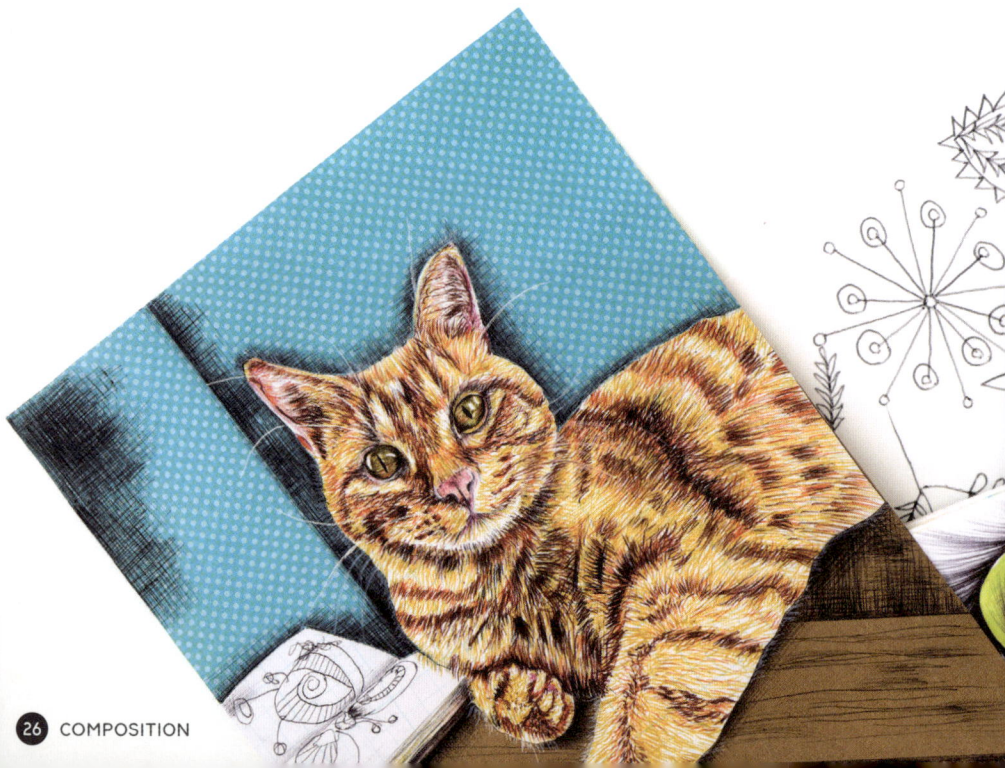

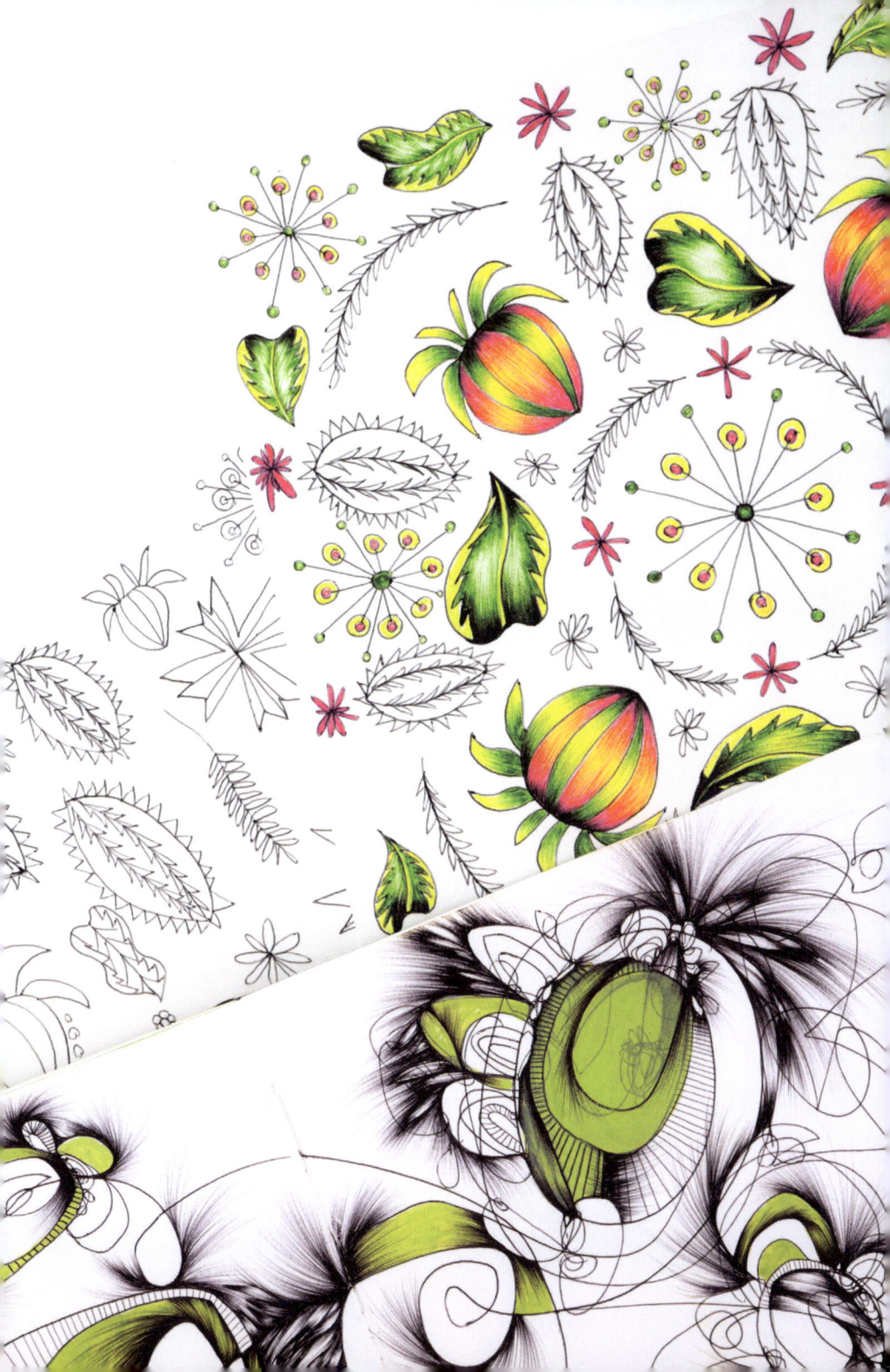

# COLOR THEORY

The color wheel is a tool that artists use to understand the relationships between colors. In simple terms, it illustrates why some colors look good together and others don't. Utilizing the color wheel to choose a palette of colors gives artwork a greater level of sophistication.

## The color wheel

The classic wheel has 12 colors, divided into three categories.

1. **Primary colors:** red, yellow, and blue. Aptly named, these are the three colors from which all others are derived. If you've done any painting or have experience with four-color printing, you'll know that this is not really true. For instance, mixing magenta and yellow will give you a great red.

2. **Secondary colors:** orange, green, and violet. These are made by mixing two primary colors together. Add red to yellow and you get orange, mix blue and yellow to make green, and mix yellow with blue to get violet.

3. **Tertiary colors:** These are made by mixing one primary and one secondary color together. These are colors with two names, like yellow-orange and blue-violet.

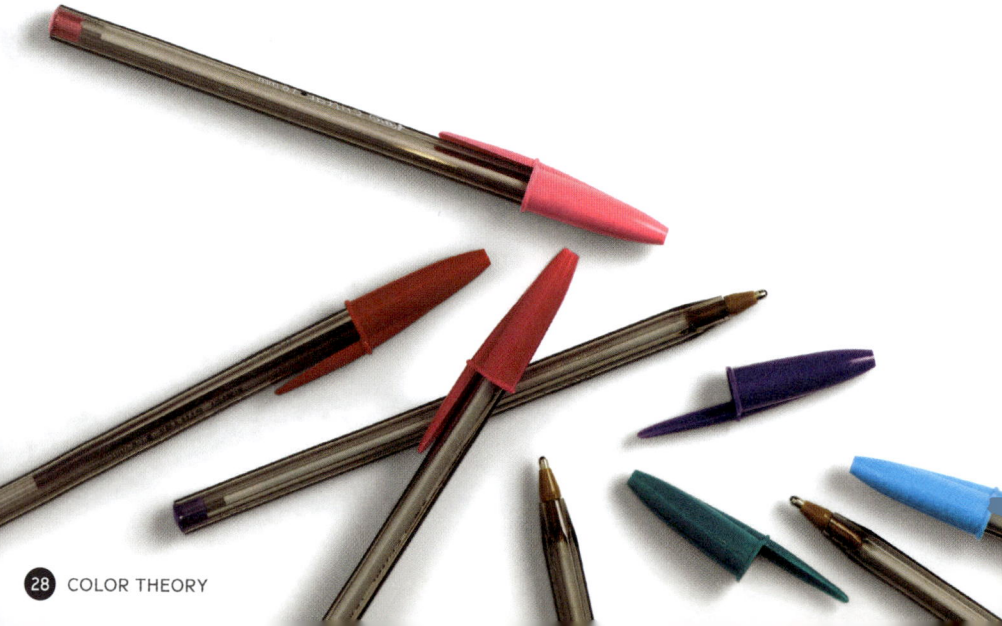

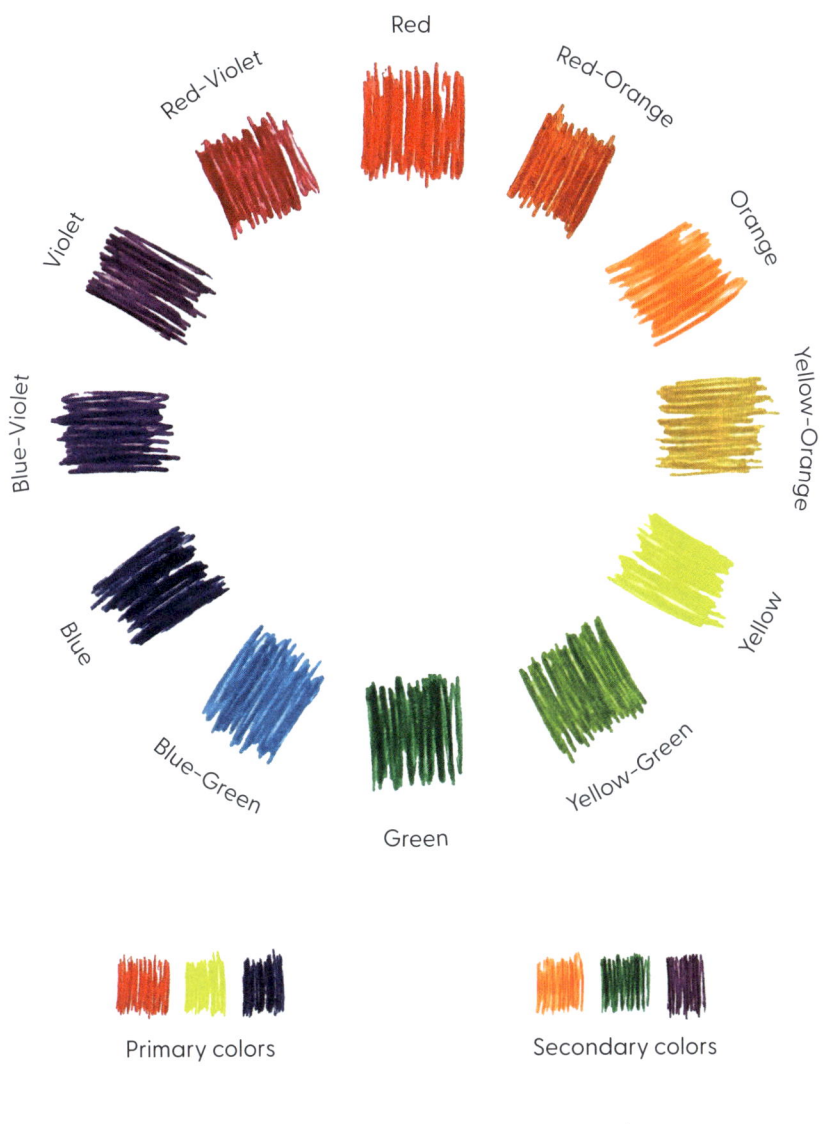

Red

Red-Violet

Red-Orange

Violet

Orange

Blue-Violet

Yellow-Orange

Blue

Yellow

Blue-Green

Yellow-Green

Green

Primary colors

Secondary colors

Tertiary colors

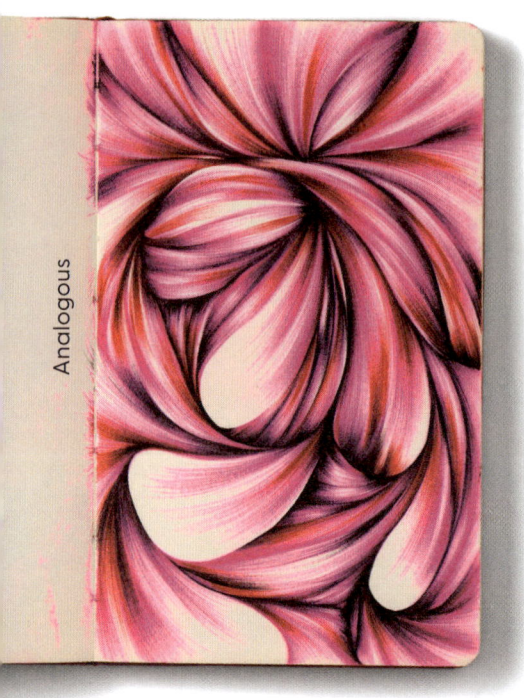

Analogous

## Classic color schemes

A color scheme is a collection of colors that have a relationship on the color wheel. Colors within a color scheme work well together and have a harmonious, pleasing look.

**Monochromatic:** When one single color is mixed with white (creating a tint), with black (creating a shade), or with gray (creating a tone). As there are no white or gray ballpoints, a monochromatic color scheme uses various versions of one color plus black. A monochromatic pen drawing could also mean using one single pen or using various versions of the same color.

**Analogous:** Two or three colors that are next to each other on the color wheel and blend together easily. As there are only a finite number of ballpoint ink colors, monochromatic and analogous color schemes can be pretty similar.

**Complementary:** Colors that are across from one another on the color wheel. Complements can be tricky to use as they are opposites on the color wheel and don't easily mix together.

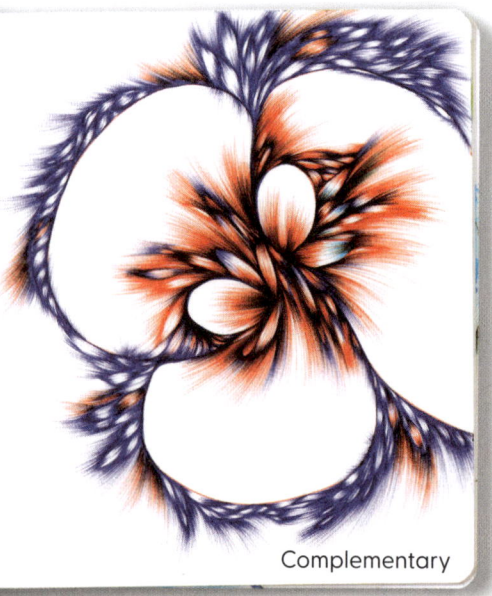

Complementary

**Triad:** Three colors that create a triangle on the color wheel. The primary colors of red, yellow, and blue make a triad as do the secondary colors of green, violet, and orange.

## Gold, black, and brown

For our purposes, gold, black, and brown are neutral colors, meaning they can work with any color scheme. All of them should be used sparingly (especially black) as they can easily overtake other colors and/or make colors look muddy.

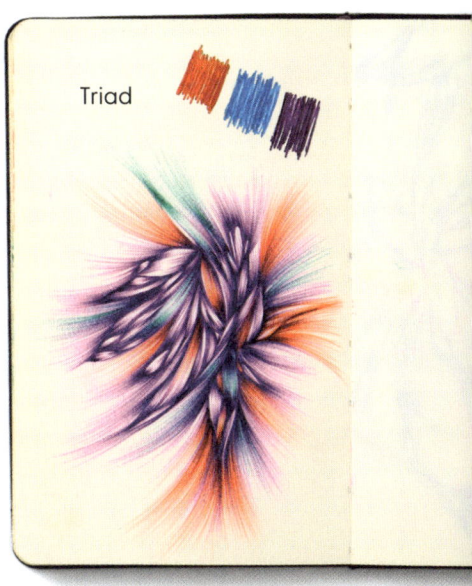

Triad

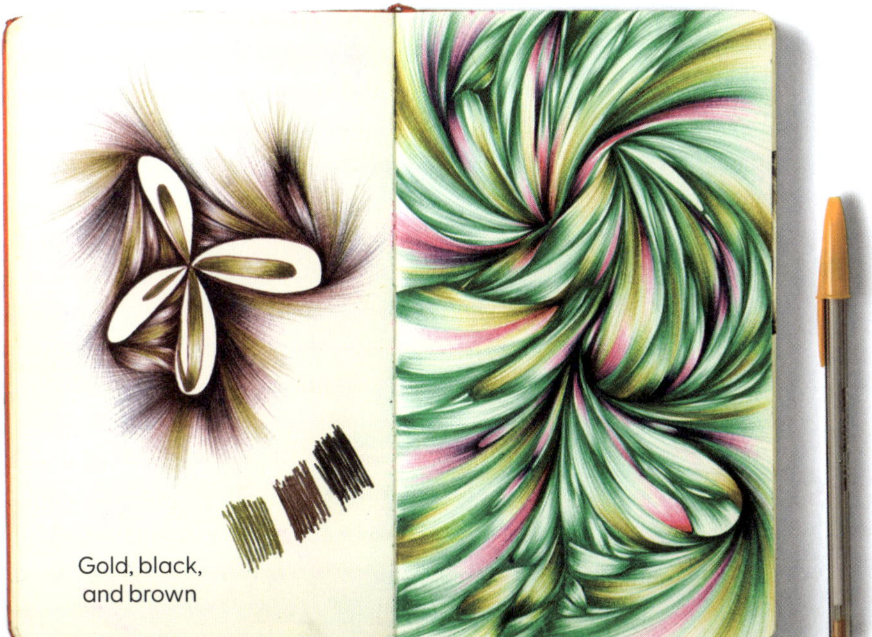

Gold, black, and brown

# BLENDING COLOR

Blending colors with ballpoint is quite like blending with colored pencils. By layering colors over the top of one another, new colors and values are created. Unlike colored pencils, there is a limited range of pen ink colors available, so blending is important to broaden the range. To keep colors from becoming muddy, blend only two to three colors at a time.

## Analogous colors

Blending analogous colors together is quite simple. As they are next to each other on the color wheel and have a color in common, they mix easily.

Start with the lighter of the two colors to create a transition from light to dark, keeping the transition on the light side overall. With a second, darker color, add another layer of ink over the top of the light. End this transition sooner than the first so that the end of the blend is just the initial color. It's also helpful to slightly vary the end point of the lines to avoid an abrupt change from one color to the other. Work back over the top of the whole shape in the lighter color and continue alternating colors until you've achieved a smooth, even change from one color to the next.

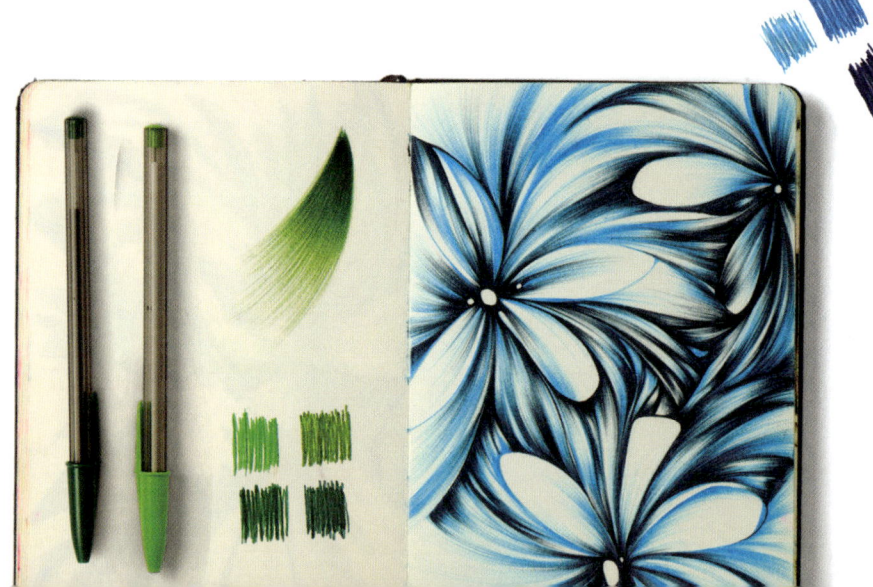

## Complementary colors

Approach blending complementary colors differently than other color combinations. As they will create brown if layered over the top of each other, work complementary colors next to each other or across from one another, and occasionally leave some white space in between them. Sparingly layer them over one another to create a darker value, and to create interest and variety.

Using one of the complements much more than the other is another way to avoid muddy blends. I will sometimes fill in a whole page with my dominant color and then go back in with the complement to create accents.

Experiment with the order you mix complements. For instance, mixing orange on top of blue makes a slightly unappealing brown. If blue is layered on top of orange, however, a more pleasing blue-green is created.

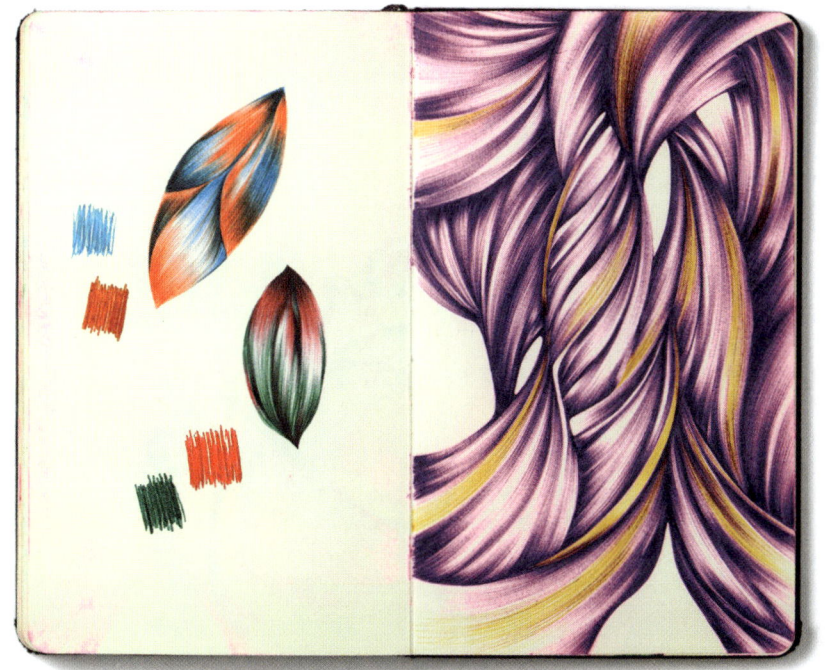

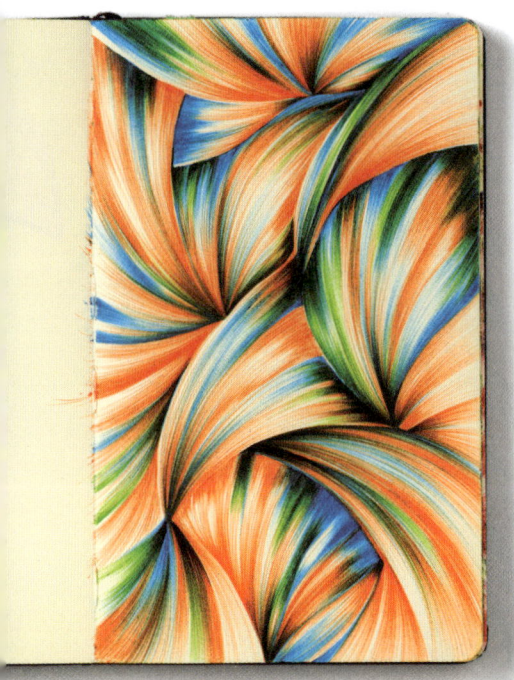

## Triad colors

You might find that blending triadic colors is easier than working with complements. As they are a step closer to each other on the color wheel, they blend together with a bit more ease, but it's quite time consuming. It's like making three drawings on top of one another, and that takes time.

When working with multiple colors, it's important to have a dominant color. In simple terms, use one color more than you use any of the others in the composition. Having a dominant color helps to create a sense of unity in your drawing.

Layer all three colors together to create the darkest values in the drawing. Overmixing will muddy up the drawing, so layer all three colors sparingly. There may be less white paper showing in triadic drawings, but I try to leave some for a greater range of value.

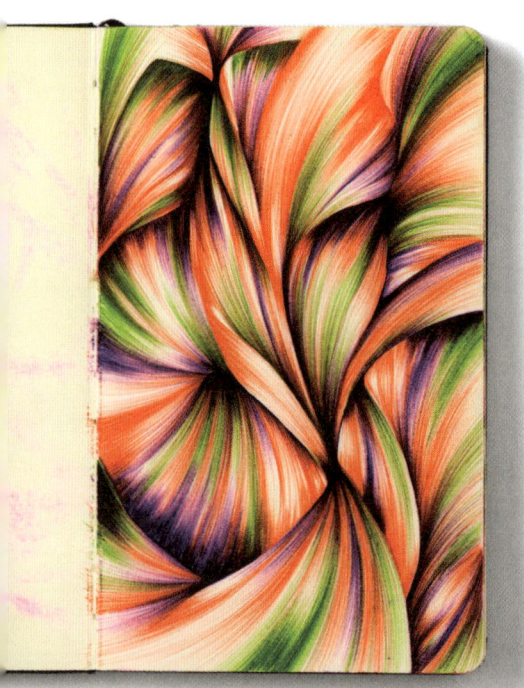

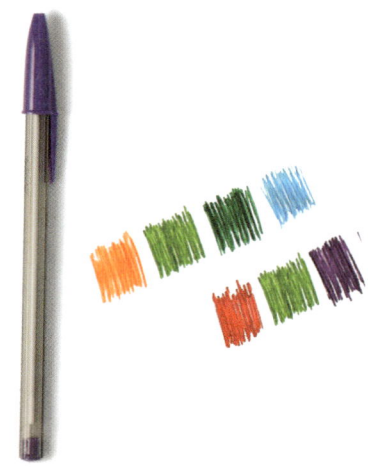

## Black and brown

Black and brown can be layered with any color. Black will darken and brown will neutralize, making a color appear less vibrant.

Brown helps to broaden your range of colors and is particularly helpful when portraying realistic subject matter. Adding brown to a pure color will make it recede into space and is helpful in creating subtle shifts in value.

Black is pretty magical. It doesn't muddy up the other colors layered underneath it. Instead, it sits on top and makes a rich, velvety dark. It's good for covering up problem areas in a drawing. A rogue blob of ink or a wavy edge are no match for black ink. Black is best used in small doses as it can easily overwhelm a composition and swallow up all the colors around it.

## Working with yellow

As a rule, it's best to start a multicolor drawing with the lightest color in your palette. When working with yellow, this is not the case. Yellow is so light and bright that you'll end up wasting ink, so add yellow towards the middle or end of the drawing. It's okay to lose the white of your paper when you're working with a bright color like yellow or even bright orange. The yellow can function as the lightest value in place of the white of the paper. As long as you pair the yellow or orange with medium values and rich darks, you'll still achieve depth and dimension.

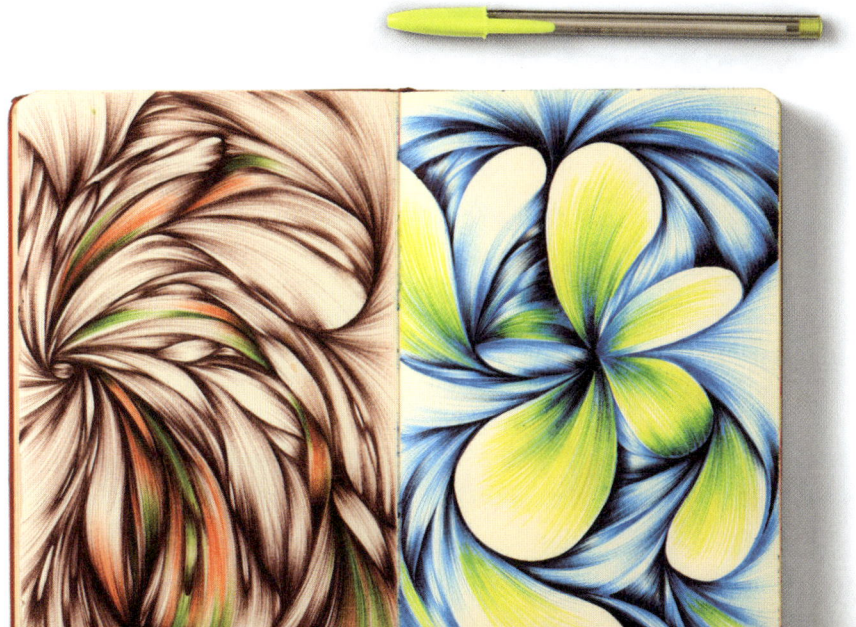

# DEALING WITH MISTAKES

It's inevitable. Mistakes are going to happen when you draw with pens. A big blob of ink might show up where you don't want it, you're not pleased with a section of your drawing, or you go too dark somewhere. I try my best to embrace these happy accidents and incorporate them into my drawing. But sometimes, I just can't live with that mistake, so I've developed a few techniques to correct them.

## 1. Ink blobs

Ink has a tendency to build up on the point of ballpoints and can create blobs of ink on your paper. Even when you're diligent about wiping the point, it's bound to happen sometimes. I have found that this occurs most with wide-point pens and less with refillable and fine-point pens. The simplest way to hide an errant blob is to cover it with more ink. When my green pen leaked on this drawing **(1a)**, I stopped and wiped away the build up of ink on the ballpoint. Then I went back into the drawing with the same green pen and covered it up **(1b)**.

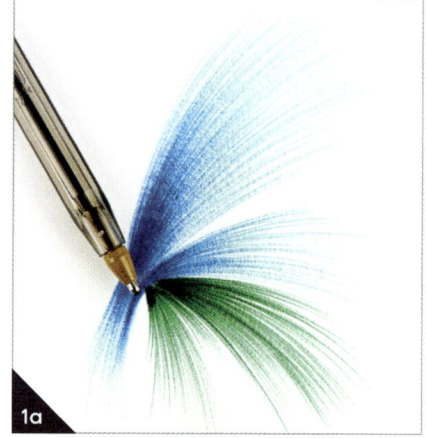

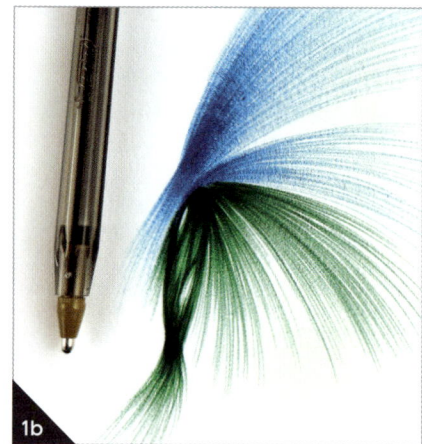

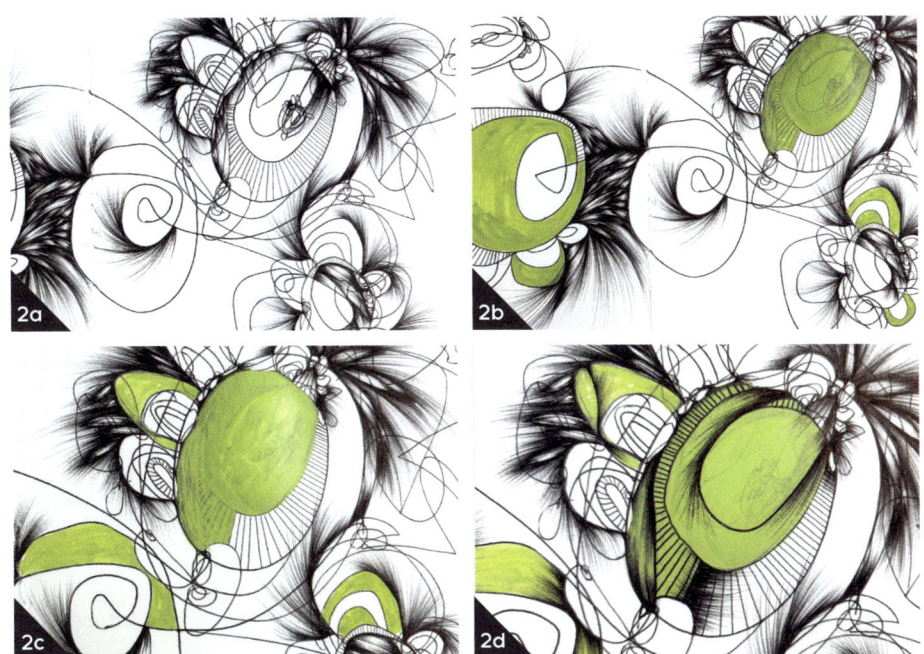

## 2. Acrylic ink

If going darker isn't an option, try acrylic ink to obscure undesirable areas. Acrylic ink is a fluid version of acrylic paint that easily accepts ballpoint. As it's slightly transparent, mix some white ink into your color so that it covers more opaquely. A light- or medium-value acrylic ink color will be best if you intend to draw with pens on top of the ink. I suggest using a color instead of straight white ink, as it's doubtful that the white of the ink will match the white of the paper, so it could draw more attention to that area than you'd like.

In my example, I wasn't fond of what I'd done in the top right corner **(2a)**.

I started to cover it with an olive green acrylic ink. To make the green seem more intentional and balanced, I added some other areas of green around the drawing **(2b)**.

As the area I was trying to cover was saturated with pen, I needed to add more than one coat of the acrylic ink **(2c)**.

Once the ink was fully dry, I continued to draw over the top with a pen. To fully incorporate the green ink into the drawing, I added pen over the top of most of the painted areas **(2d)**.

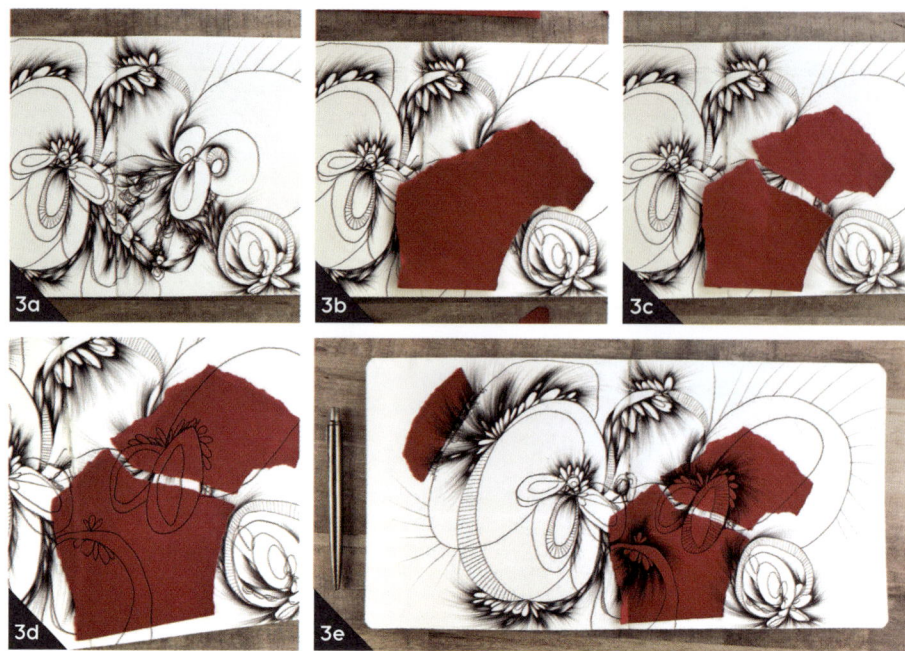

## 3. Collage

Collage paper can be used much like the acrylic ink, but with less mess. In this drawing, I wasn't happy with the area in the middle at the bottom **(3a)**.

To cover this undesirable area, I chose a contrasting paper that would accept pen. I like to rip the edges of the paper to give it more of an organic look **(3b)**.

I created a patch to cover the offending area, but it felt too overbearing, so I ripped it into two pieces before adhering it to the page with a glue stick **(3c)**.

To tie the collaged element into the existing drawing, I carried some of the lines and shapes from the original drawing onto the collage **(3d)**.

Just like with the paint, I added another piece of the red paper to create some balance. I continued embellishing until the collage pieces felt unified with the rest of the drawing **(3e)**.

### TOP TIP

If you can't resolve your drawing with one of these methods, that's okay. Walk away and come back to it later, or just abandon it and move on. Believe me, every artist has a graveyard of "failed" drawings. Use those pieces as an opportunity for learning and growth.

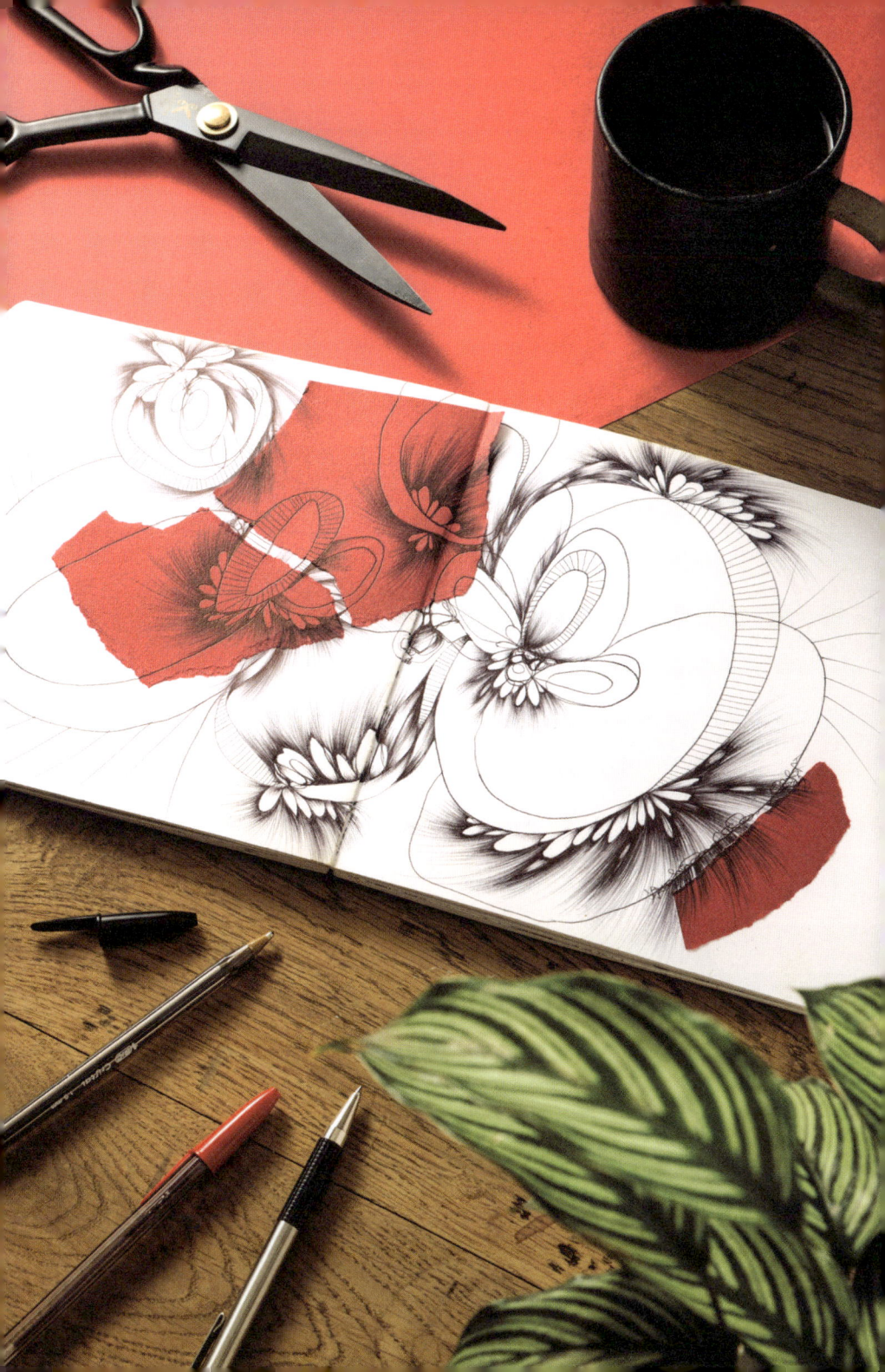

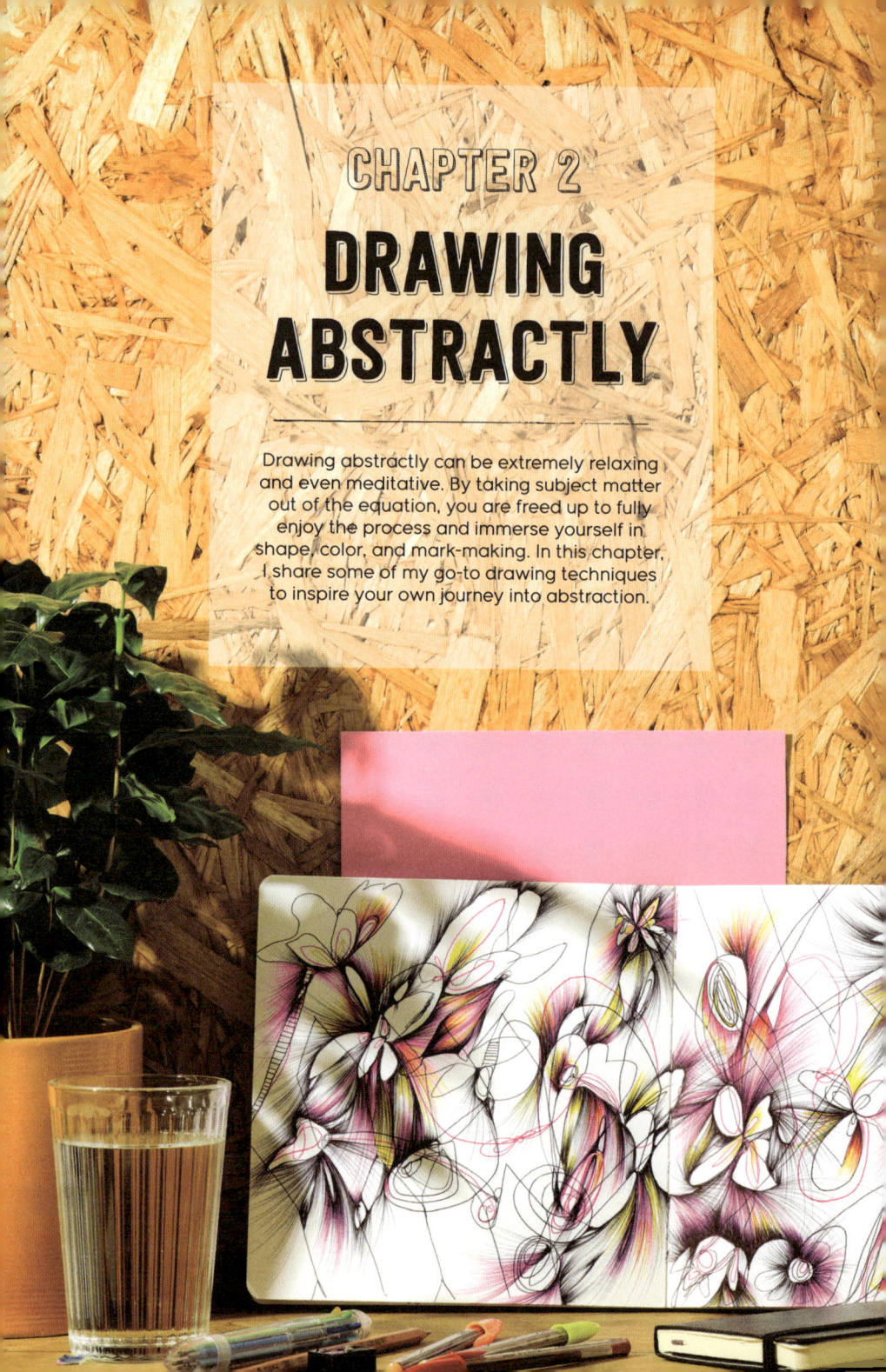

# CHAPTER 2
# DRAWING ABSTRACTLY

Drawing abstractly can be extremely relaxing and even meditative. By taking subject matter out of the equation, you are freed up to fully enjoy the process and immerse yourself in shape, color, and mark-making. In this chapter, I share some of my go-to drawing techniques to inspire your own journey into abstraction.

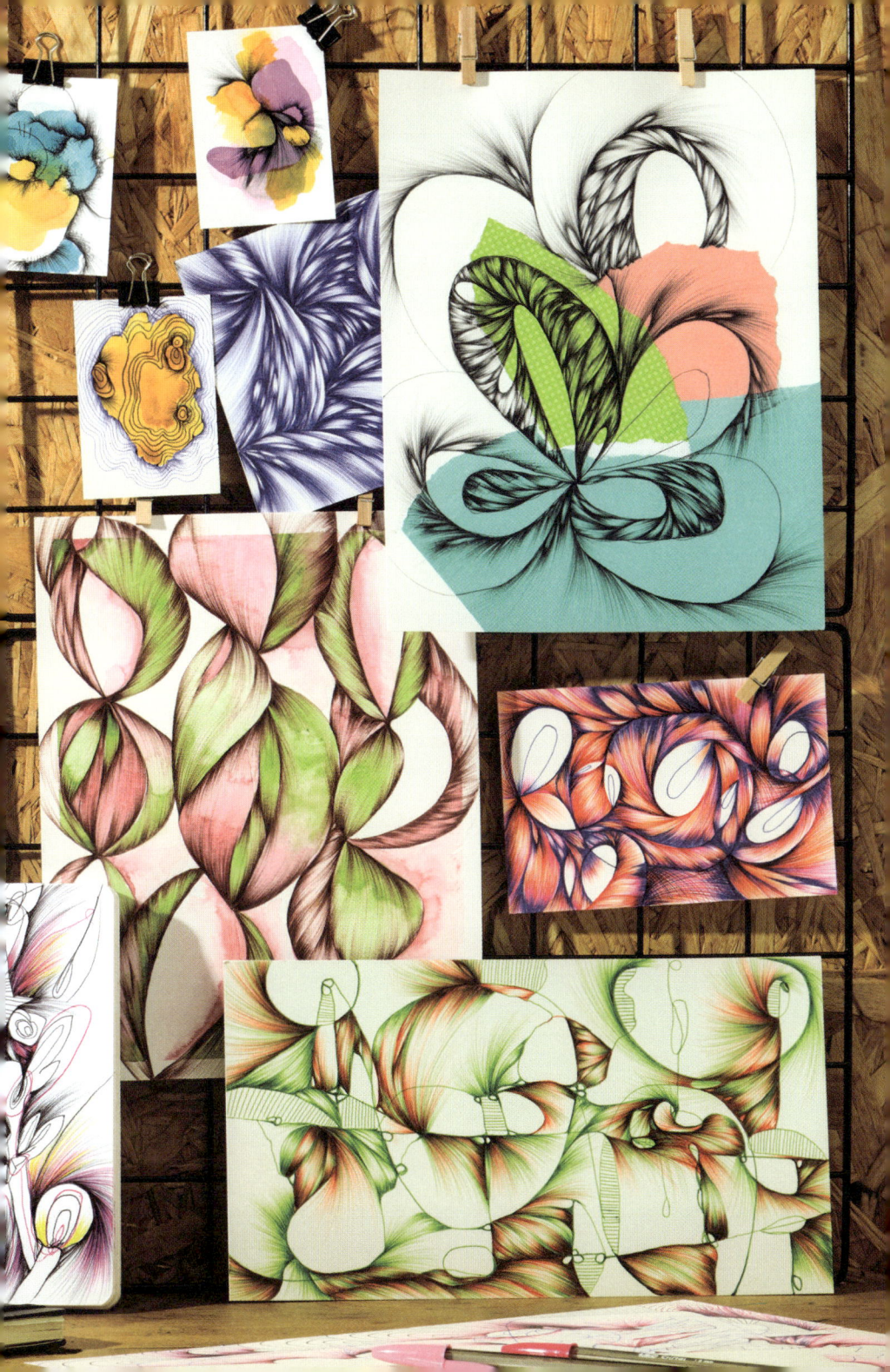

# ONE-COLOR ABSTRACT

In this exercise, I share my signature shading technique using one color. This is a good way to practice creating gradual, smooth gradients. It can be a time-consuming technique, so I advise working small. If you're just getting started with ballpoint, consider using a traditional color of blue, black, or red. The ink is more viscous and will flow a bit more smoothly.

## YOU WILL NEED

- 5 x 5in (13 x 13cm) smooth paper
- Blue wide-point pen
- Scratch paper
- Pencil (optional)
- Paper towel (optional)

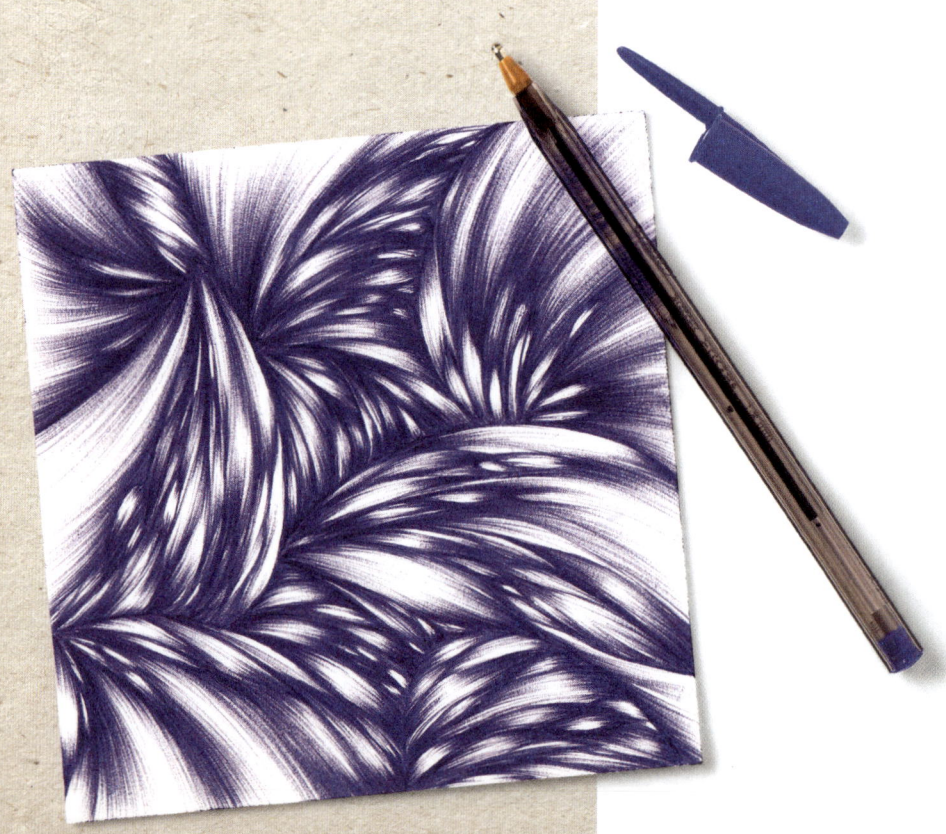

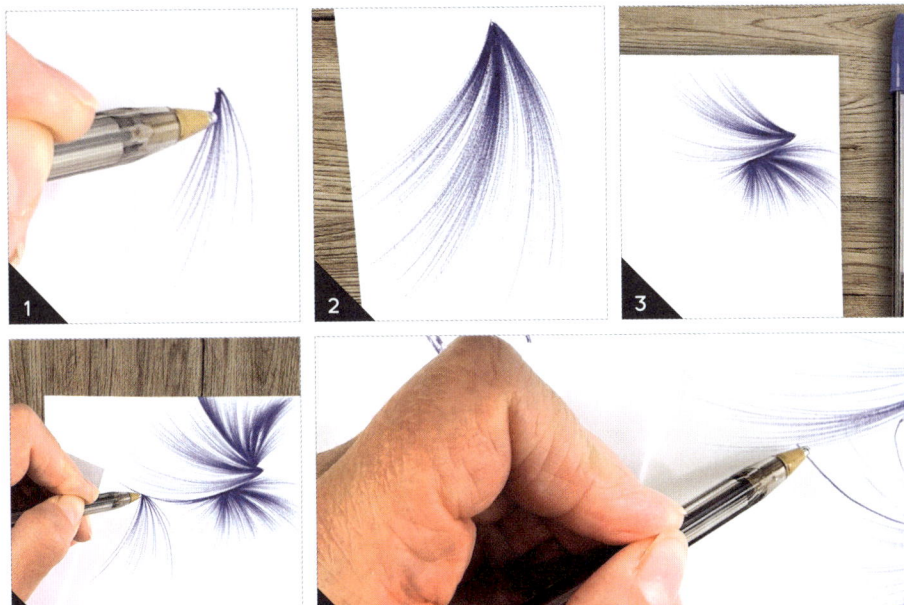

1. Place a scratch piece of paper under your drawing hand and make your first marks somewhere off-center. If jumping in with ink seems daunting, lightly draw a fan shape with a pencil.

2. Create a transition from light to dark by slowly building up light layers of ink. To avoid ink building up, regularly roll the point of the pen on a piece of scratch paper or on some paper towel.

3. Turn your paper and start a new transition up against the edge of your first transition. Build a gradient, slowly fading that dark edge to the white of the paper.

4. Continue building off the existing shapes with more fan-shaped transitions. Vary the size and amount of dark and light in each to create interest.

Keep the scratch paper underneath your hand throughout the drawing process so as not to smudge the ink underneath.

5. When the end of a fan shape touches another, shade the opposite end dark and gradually fade to light. The goal is to seamlessly blend this new transition into the existing one.

## TOP TIP

Work dark values up against light edges/shapes to create contrast and depth. Keep your drawing light, as you can always go darker and you'll preserve some of the light of the paper so that you have a full range of values in the end.

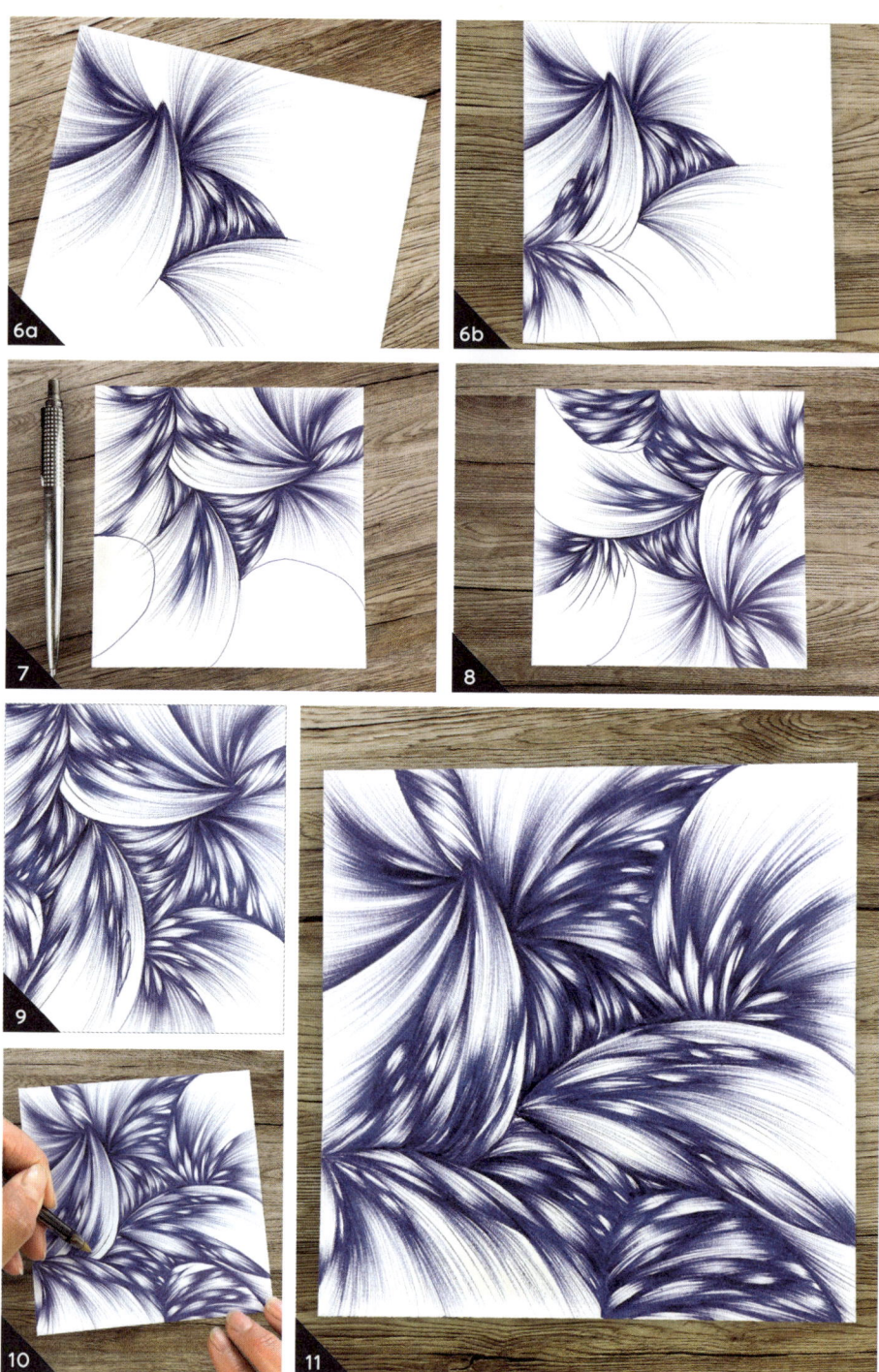

6. Add some mini transitions within the larger transitions. Draw seed-like shapes and add transitions within the seed to give it an appearance of roundness. Including these smaller shapes adds interest and detail.

7. When you're about halfway through the composition, try to make a tentative plan for the remaining space. How will you divide it up so there are a variety of shapes? You can make some notes right on the drawing with pen, or use a pencil and erase the pencil lines later.

8. Once you've filled the page, turn your attention to the details. Create sharp, precise edges where one shape meets another. Try to eliminate any outlines that divide one shape from another as they spoil the illusion of depth and space. Instead of an outline, create a difference in value (also referred to as contrast).

9. If you've been hesitant to go dark in your drawing, now is the time to add dark areas. Make sure there are pockets of dark all around the composition and use them to heighten the contrast between neighboring shapes. Get your darks as dark as you can. It will make your drawing look more finished, interesting, and dimensional as you will have achieved a full range of value on the page.

10. Rich, inky darks give a drawing depth and visual appeal, but going dark on the whole drawing isn't the goal. Lighter values and some of the white of the paper will round out your composition and make it more interesting.

11. Your goal is to create a harmonious flow. As you're looking at your work, your eye should easily move around the drawing. No part should stand out too much more than the rest. A little variety is good, but you don't want any area of your drawing to look like it doesn't belong there.

## TOP TIP

Consider the drawing finished when:

* There are dark, medium, and light values interspersed all around the composition
* The edges of shapes are sharp
* Transitions from dark to light are gradual and flowing
* The composition has an overall flow, with no area standing out too much.

# MULTICOLOR ABSTRACT

Using more than one color of ink will expand your value range and create an even greater sense of depth and interest in your drawing. It's easiest to choose analogous colors or work with one color plus black. If you'd like to challenge yourself, try out a triad or a pair of complements. Here, we'll use an analogous color combination with orange as the light, magenta as the medium, and blue as the dark. If you don't have these colors, then pick whatever light, medium, and dark values work within an analogous combination.

## YOU WILL NEED

- 4 x 6in (10 x 15cm) smooth paper
- Wide-point pens in orange, magenta, and blue
- Scratch paper
- Pencil (optional)

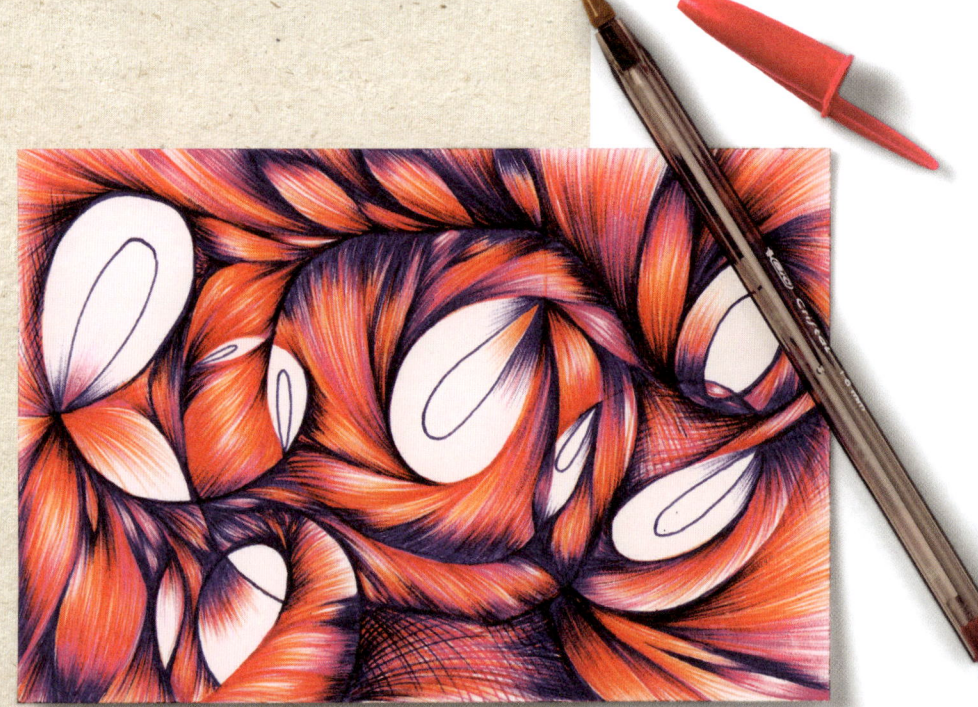

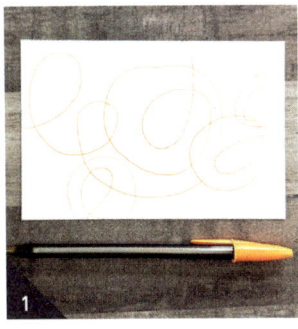

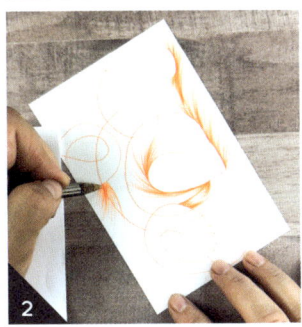

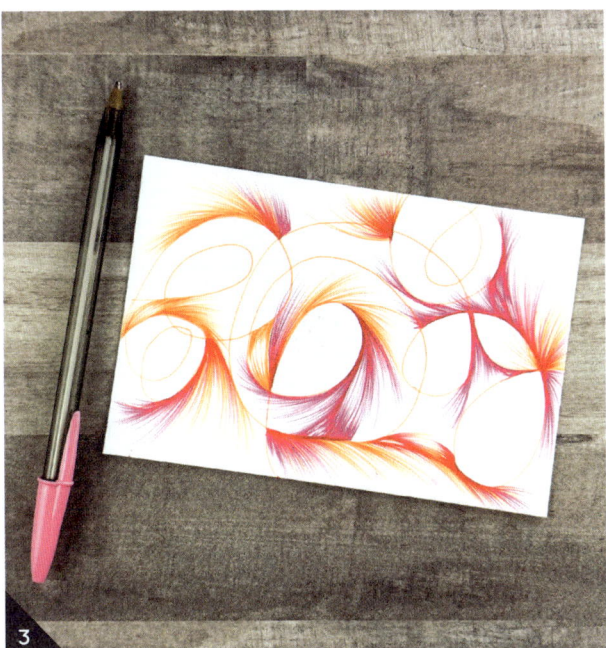

1. Start by doodling around the page in orange, the lightest color in the palette. If it seems scary to jump straight in, doodle lightly with a pencil. Loosen up your hand and without much thought, simply make marks. Try long, continuous lines that loop around the paper. Aim to quickly break up the space into some larger and smaller shapes.

2. With the scratch paper under your hand, start shading with the orange. Find shapes that are appealing and shade around them or inside of them to highlight those areas. If there are shapes that were created during the initial doodling that you don't like, simply shade over the top of them. Work your way around the format, creating transitions from light to dark, keeping it light overall.

3. Introduce magenta (or middle-value color), both on top of the orange and on its own. As the orange and magenta are analogous, they layer together easily. You can even see some color theory in action here. When layered over the top of one another, a red is created. Continue to refine the composition by covering less desirable areas and highlighting others. Work your way around the composition evenly, instead of concentrating and finishing one area at a time. That way, the drawing develops as a whole and looks more unified. Work with the magenta until you've got enough areas of color around the format or you get bored using it!

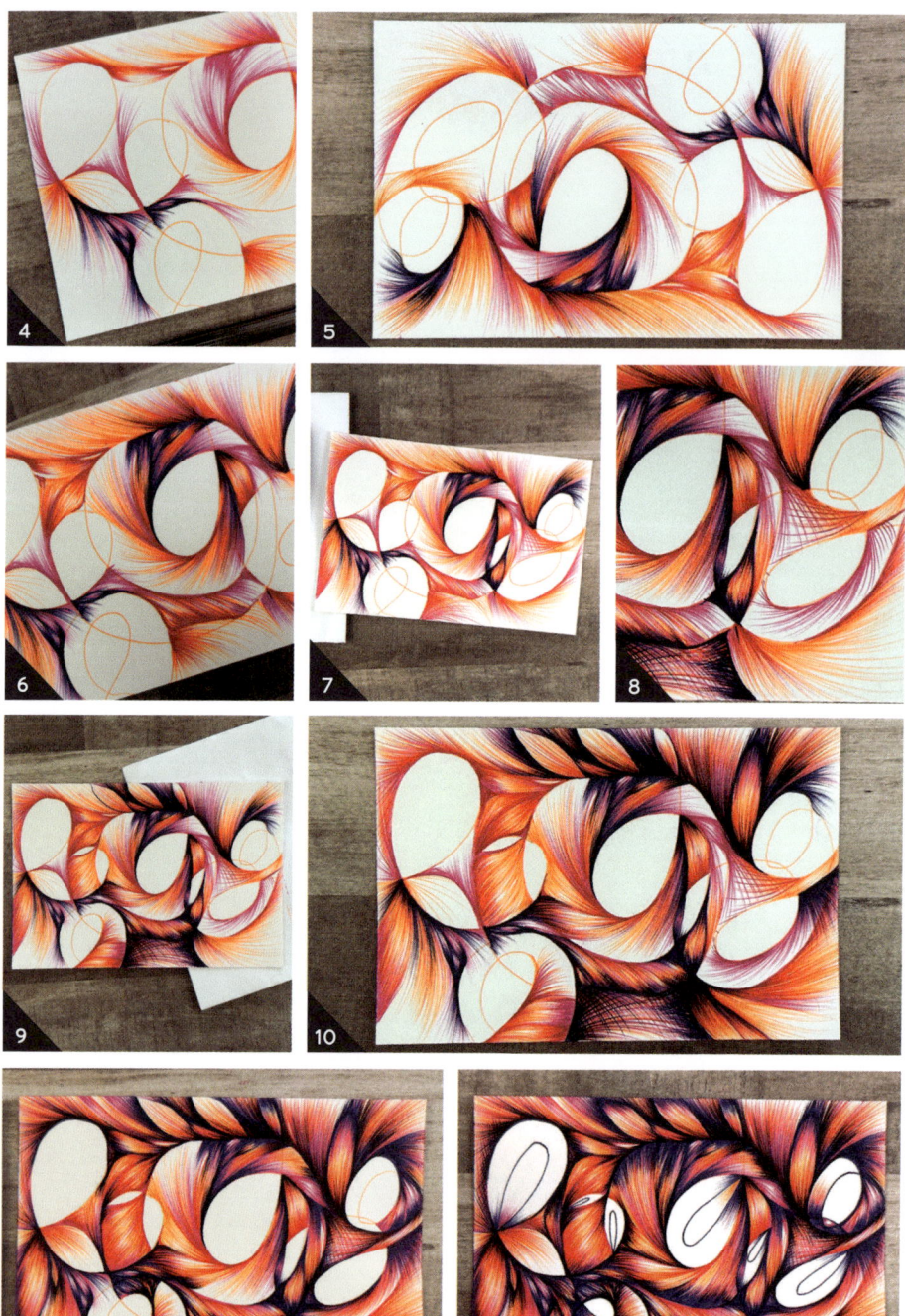

4. At this point, introduce the blue (or darkest color pen). Add just a little at a time, so there is still room for some change and fluidity in the composition. Because they are analogous, I mainly layer the blue over the magenta and less so over the orange to prevent the orange and blue creating a brown hue. When you add in that dark, the light colors start popping off the page and a sense of space begins to emerge.

5. Once a little of the blue has been introduced, start to bounce back and forth between all three colors. Begin to develop areas of the drawing you find interesting while still surveying the drawing as a whole from time to time.

6. Play with shapes so they appear to weave over and under each other. Add dark values to make shapes fall back and underneath another form. Then the shapes on top are either a light or a medium.

7. As you continue filling in the space, work on creating a focal point. In this drawing, the focal point is the white tear drop shape that has been accented by the dark values. Before carrying on, make a rough plan about where you'll retain white space around the format. Think of this as the notes phase. Don't worry about making everything perfect and polished, instead you are building up the composition, so everything will eventually flow together.

8. Repeat patterns that you like. As I was working, a cross-hatch pattern developed in one of the corners of the drawing. I liked what was happening, so I decided to repeat that in a few other areas, so that it looked intentional.

9. The blue has been used sparingly until this point, but now that the composition is solidified, you can add more in. Use it to pull the composition together, as it leads the viewer's eye around the drawing. Use it to clean up wobbly edges, obscure mistakes, and create contrast between overlapping shapes. When using blue, try to be more diligent about keeping scratch paper under your drawing hand to prevent smudging. It's much more difficult to obscure the blue than it is the magenta or orange.

10. If there are large areas of color that need some interest, add some smaller shapes. You can use the seed-like shapes as in the One-Color Abstract or whatever comes naturally and is part of your drawing vocabulary.

11. Once you've filled the space, it's time to create an overall sense of balance. Make sure there are dark, medium, and light values interspersed throughout the drawing. Clean up uneven edges and rough transitions and make sure there is contrast between overlapping shapes.

12. To give more interest to the negative spaces, add in some lines. Then it's time to call it quits. It's easy to continue to obsess over every edge and transition. (I still look at this now and find things I could change.) But it's time to call this one finished and admire your work.

# MIXED MEDIA: COLLAGE

Collage is an easy way to add color to a drawing. Thin, smooth paper with a matte finish works best. Use flat-colored paper or something with a subtle pattern that won't compete with your drawing. If you're looking for specific colors, check out the scrapbook paper section at the craft store. Thrift stores are great places to pick up collage materials on the cheap, especially if you're looking for something with patina.

## YOU WILL NEED

- 8 x 10in (20 x 25.5cm) smooth paper
- Selection of colored and/or patterned paper
- Glue stick
- Black medium-point pen
- Scissors (optional)
- Pencil (optional)

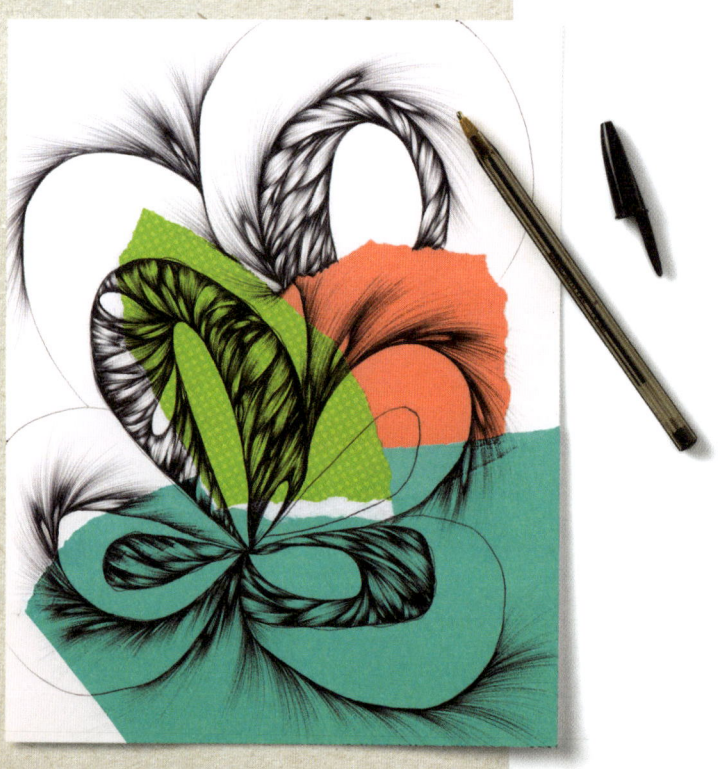

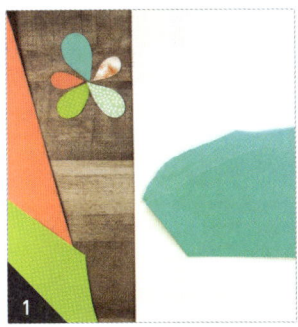

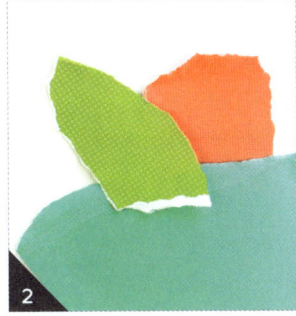

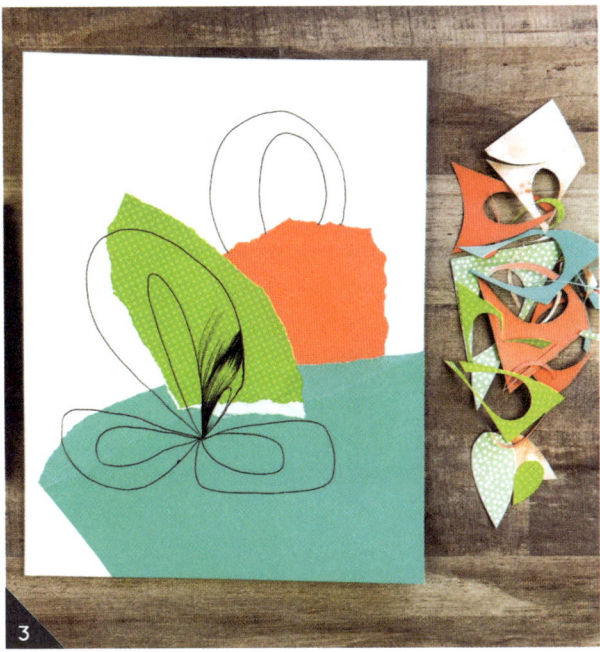

1. Choose one collage element to build your color scheme around. I started with the aqua (a blue-green) paper, and then added salmon pink (a red-orange) and a yellow-green polka dot pattern, creating a triad.

2. Cut or tear the paper into interesting shapes. Once you have some shapes you like, move them around the format until you come up with a pleasing configuration and use a glue stick to adhere them in place. While the glue dries, survey the composition and make a loose plan for the pen. What elements of the collage do you want to emphasize? Is there anything you need to obscure with ink? Where will the focal point be?

3. Using the black pen, make your first marks in response to the collage. I made some large shapes to connect the collage elements to the white background. Just make a few marks to start, so there's lots of room for experimentation and play as the composition develops.

## TOP TIP

Choose an ink color that is darker in value than the collage pieces so that the ink will be visible on top of the paper. I'm partial to black when working with collage, but use any dark ink you prefer. It's also a good idea to test the pen on each of the papers to make sure that they will accept the ink.

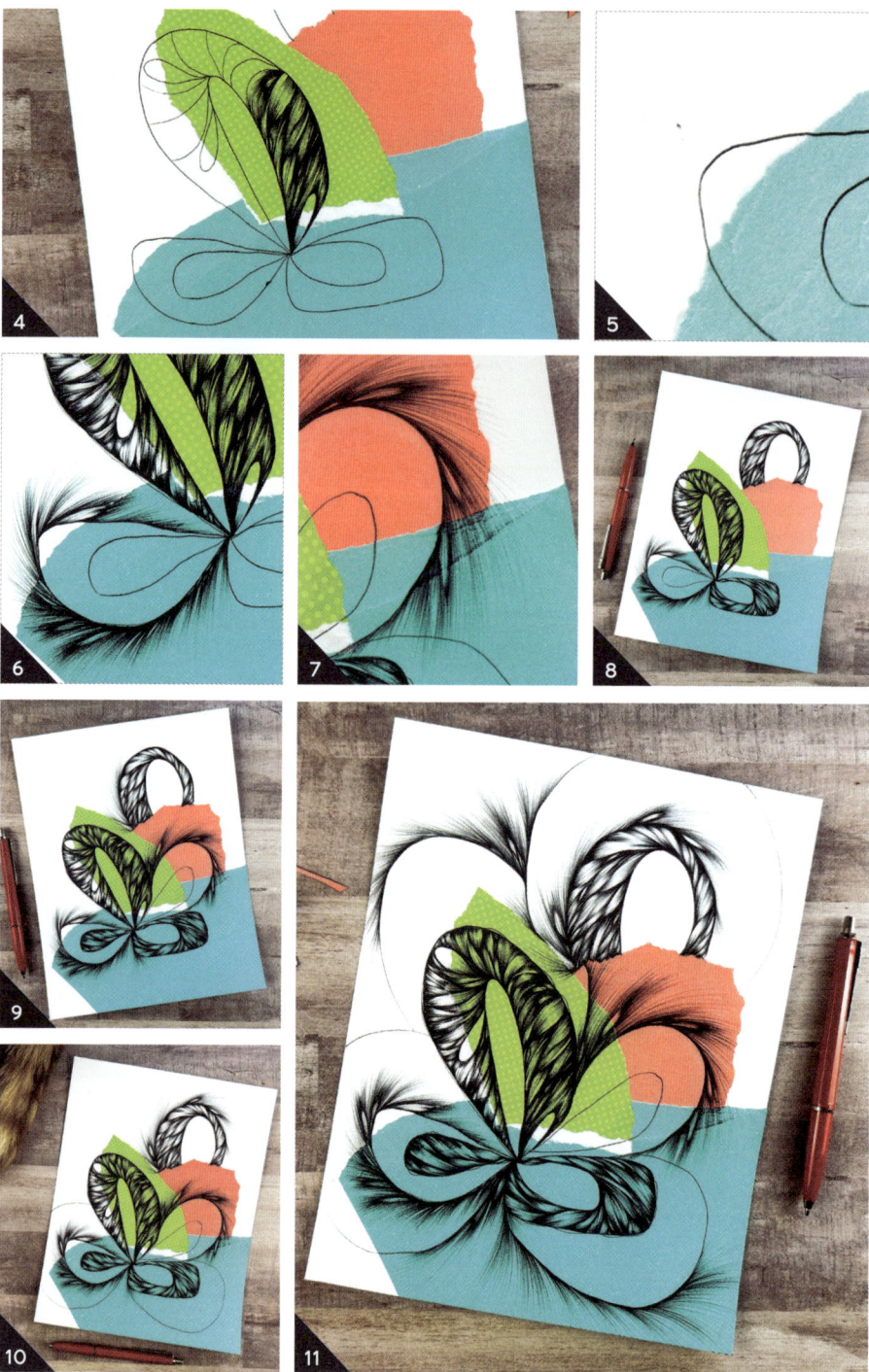

4. Start to shade in the shapes using the light to dark transition methods we've already used. I started to shade one of the petal shapes, wrapping the marks around the edges of the form. I made some light marks to plan how I would shade inside the form, and then filled the shape with many small transitions that take on a braid-like appearance.

5. If you spot smudges, don't worry as there'll be a way to deal with it (see Dealing with Mistakes in The Basics). Here, I was about to shade the next petal, I noticed a smudge of ink on the white paper.

6. To cover this smudge, I decided to shade around the outside of the petal instead of inside.

7. The torn edges of the paper will accept the ink differently than the other paper areas. Embrace it. Let it do what it does. Your transitions might not be as smooth and that's okay. Details like this create interest and personality.

8. Continue shading until you have filled in all of the drawn shapes. Now you've reached the point that I call the messy middle. It can be easy to give up at this point, as you're not sure what to do next or if you even like it enough to continue. I felt like my drawing lacked cohesion and didn't look finished.

9. To create a more unified look, go back to the basics, considering value, composition, and contrast. I added a new petal shape to make a connection between the form that flows out of the salmon-pink shape and the rest of the drawn elements. I also repeated the shading around the form in the bottom left, so this didn't look so out of place.

10. This brought more balance to the drawing, but it still needed something. I added some outlines, to give a little detail and bring some elements off the edge of the page. You'll also spot Richard the cat, who was busy helping and turns up again later in the book.

11. Stand back and review. Does it look finished? I fully intended to be done at this point, but the drawing still appeared incomplete to me. After a bit more shading around some new lines, and a little less negative space, I stepped away and called it a day.

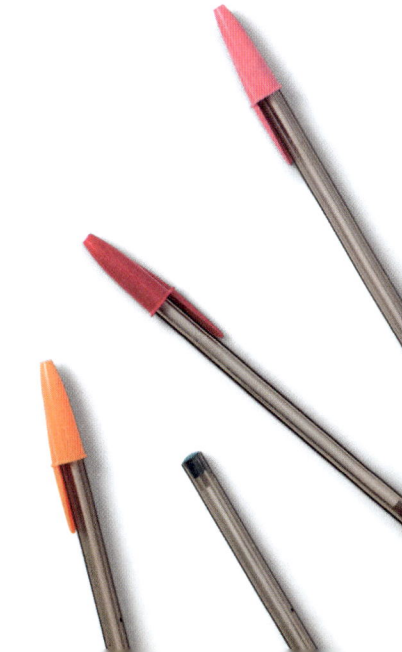

# MIXED MEDIA: ACRYLIC INK

Working small and in multiples can be extremely liberating. You're more likely to take risks and experiment if you have more than one chance to get it right. In this exercise, I'll share three quick approaches to working small with artist trading cards (ATCs), acrylic ink, and pen. I love using acrylic ink as a starting point, as the composition is basically made for you. It can take away some of the anxiety of staring at a blank page. Simply respond to the shapes that you see in the ink.

## YOU WILL NEED

- Several blank ATCs
- Acrylic ink in several colors
- Soft watercolor brushes
- Paint palette (to mix colors)
- Medium- or fine-point pens
- Glue stick (optional)

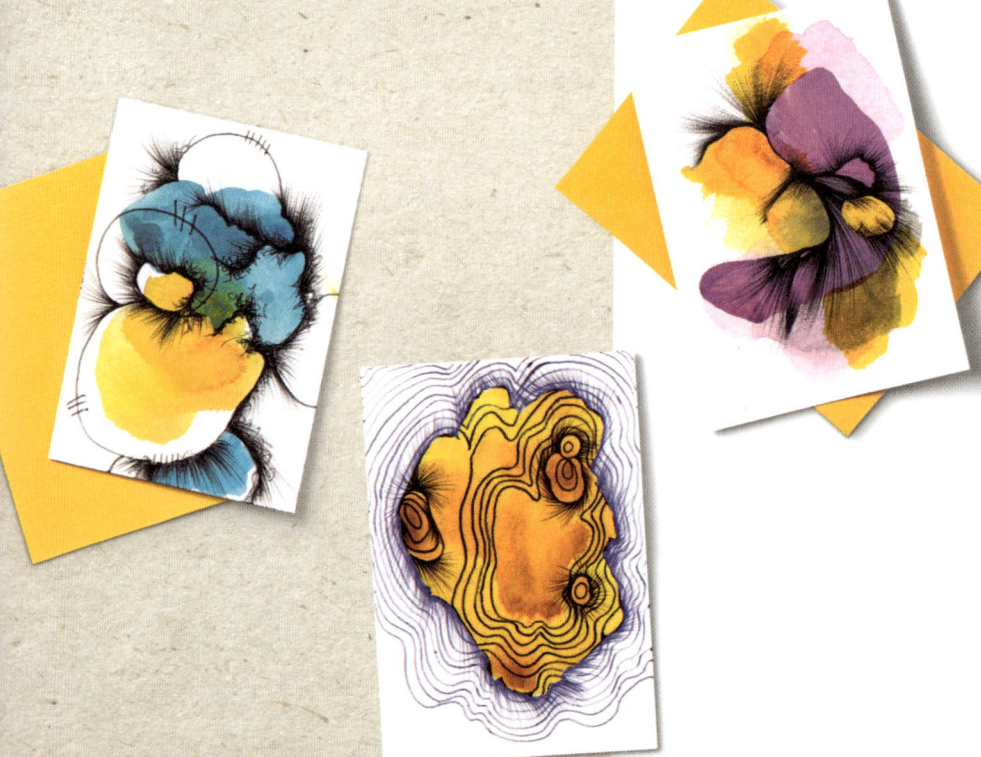

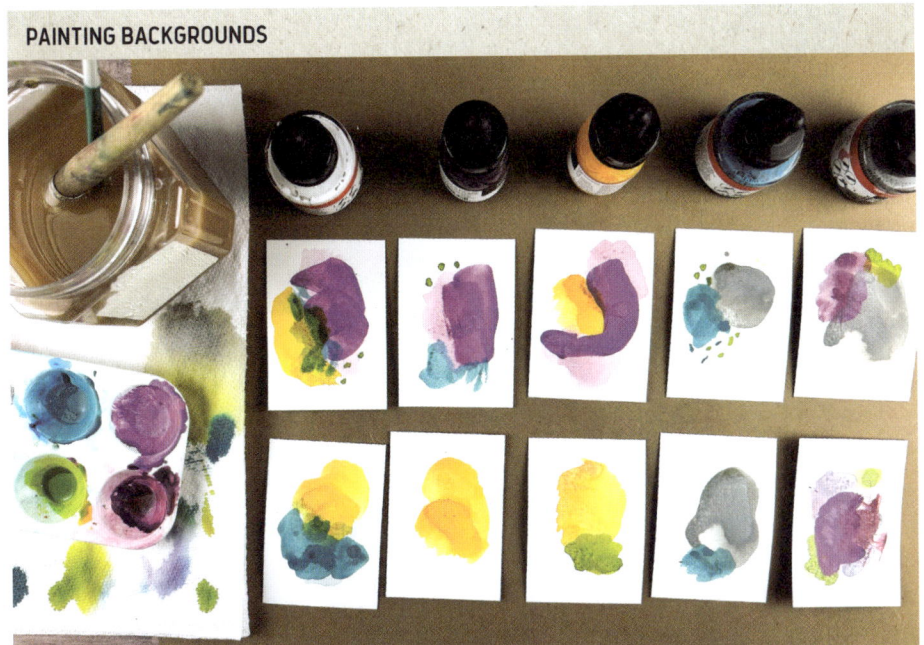

## Painting backgrounds

1. Choose or mix three to four colors of acrylic ink that will serve as background colors for your drawings. If you're using a dark blue, violet, or green, mix some white into the ink so that the pen will be visible on top of the ink.

2. Create marks on the ATCs with the acrylic ink. Have fun moving paint around the paper without much thought. Loosen up your hand and just go for it! Experiment with different brushes to make different types of marks. To keep yourself loose, paint several backgrounds so you can discard the ones that you don't care for. Try to keep some white of the paper visible.

3. Once the ink has dried, choose some of your favorites to become the background for the drawings. I find it easiest to draw on top of the more simple paintings.

### TOP TIP

The only rule to making Artist Trading Cards (ATCs) is the size. They are exactly 2½ x 3½in (6.35 x 8.89cm), the same size as a baseball card. Since the late 1990s, artists have been making and trading these miniature works of art all over the world in person and through online swaps.

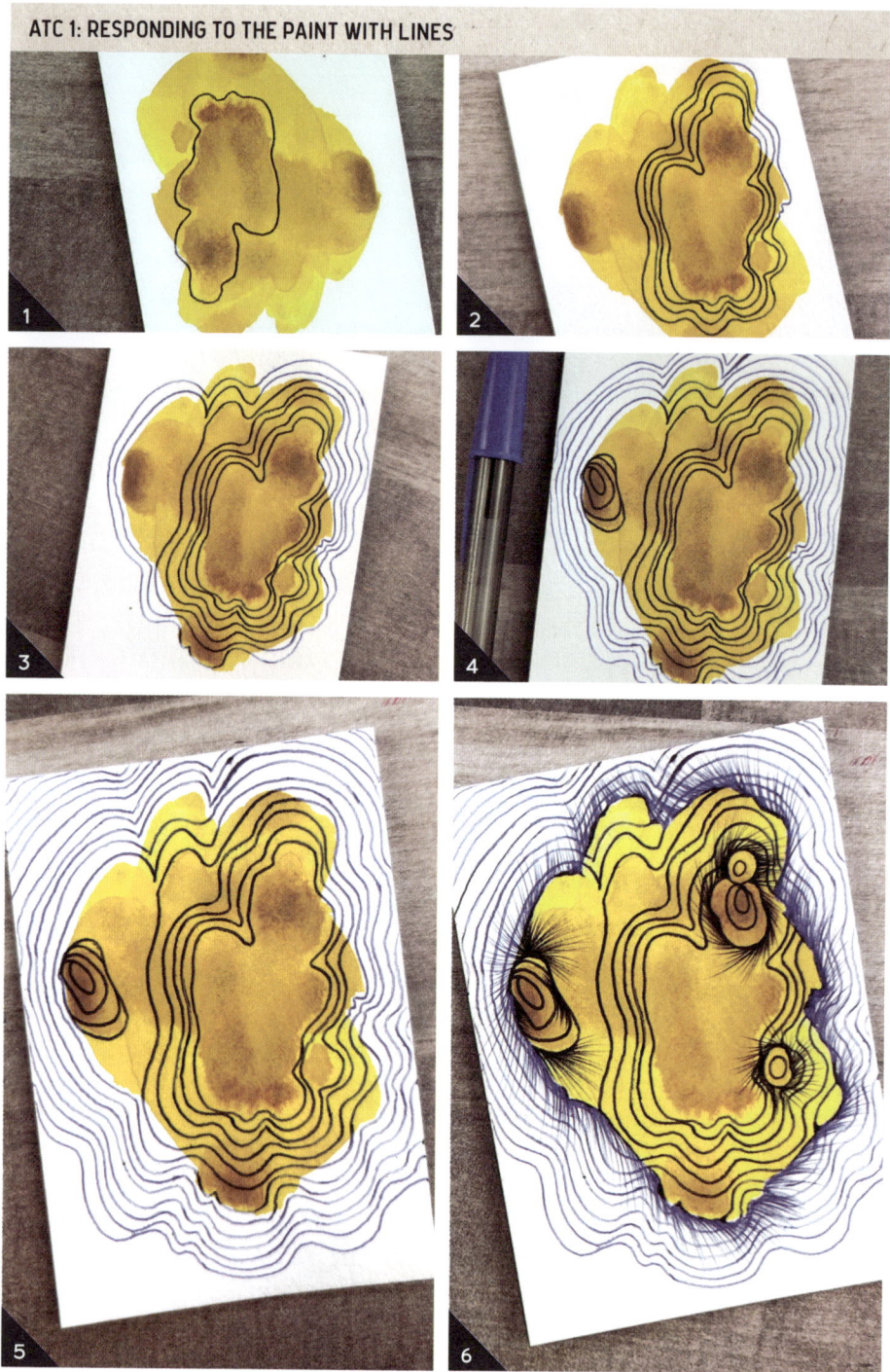

## ATC 1: Responding to the paint with lines

1. Look carefully at the painted surface and find an interesting shape. Outline that shape with a dark-colored pen (I used a blue with a medium point). Follow as closely to the edges of the ink as you'd like. I kept my line off the edge a bit so that the small detail of the bleeding paint was still visible.

2. Continue circling the shape with lines. Keep the spacing between the lines the same or vary it from line to line.

3. When you reach the edges of the acrylic ink, stop and survey the drawing to determine a focal point. In my drawing, two large negative spaces in the middle of the ink spot were competing for attention.

4. To create one clear focal point, I added some circles to the negative space on the left, drawing more attention there.

5. Keep going until you've filled most of the card with lines. The more lines drawn, the more interesting the composition becomes. I chose to leave a little white space at the bottom to give the eye a place to rest.

6. Finish up by adding some dark values and a bit more detail to the composition. I added some more circular shapes and shaded around some of them with a curved hatch stroke.

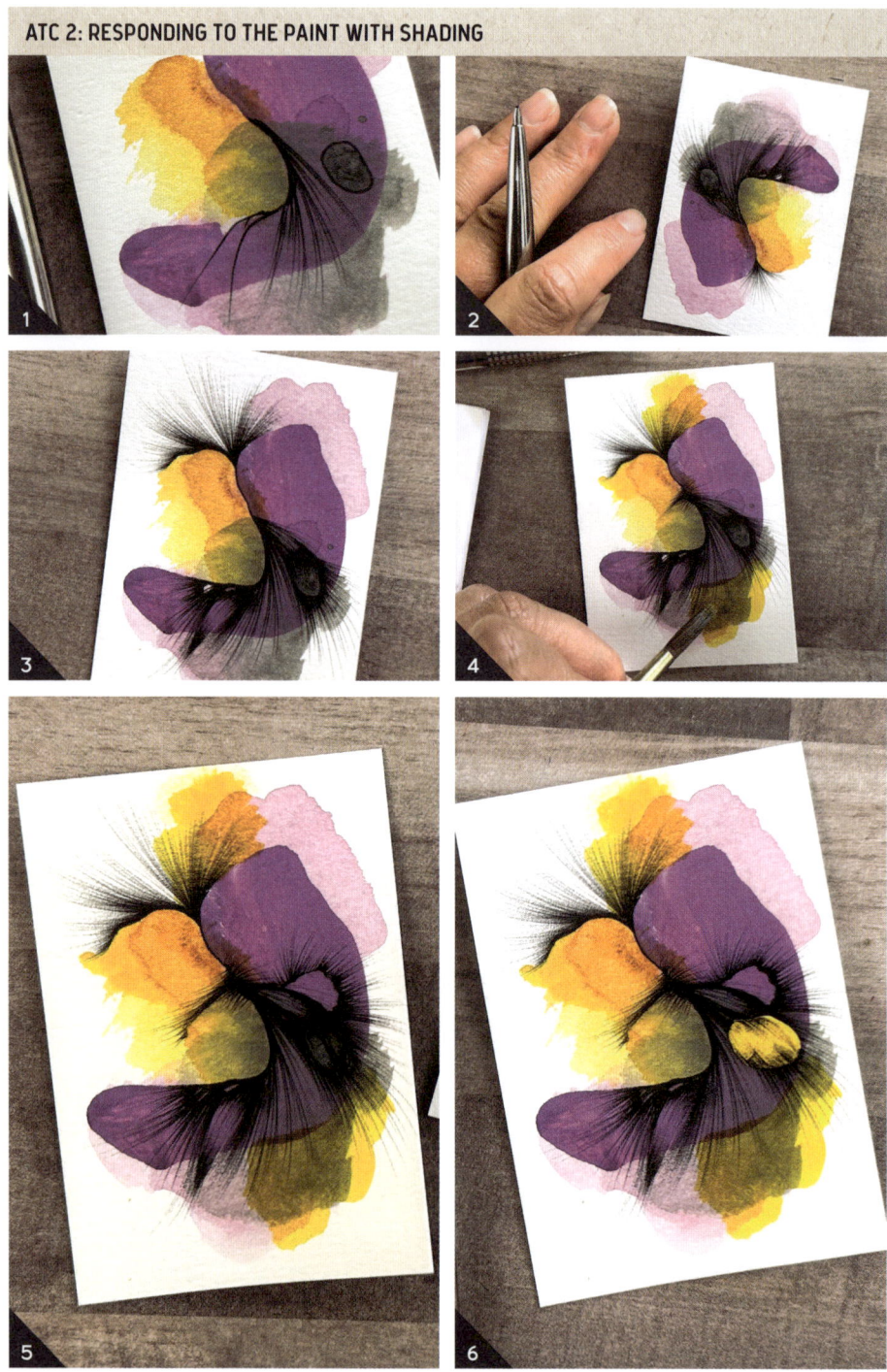

## ATC 2: Responding to the paint with shading

1. Look carefully at the ink and find an interesting shape or two to highlight with some smooth shading. In my example, I started to emphasize the yellow form by shading around it. I also outlined the gray dot in the middle of the violet form.

2. Continue shading around the forms you'd like to highlight in your composition. If you haven't already, try to determine the orientation of your drawing—turn your drawing around to see which way is the most appealing to you.

3. Add more shading to further emphasize your focal point shape. I added more shading to the opposite side of the yellow form, which started to visually lift the form above the other shapes.

4. If the composition feels unbalanced or uninspiring, you may need to add more ink. It bothered me that the yellow only appeared in one place, so I added it in two more areas and it was instantly more balanced.

5. Once the ink is dry, you can continue to shade with the pen. If there are areas you aren't happy with and adding more pen isn't going to help, consider making a patch. I felt the area around the gray spot was murky, so I painted some yellow on some extra paper, cut it out, and glued it into place.

6. Allow the glue to dry, then as a final touch, add some shading in or around the patch to make it blend in with the existing drawing.

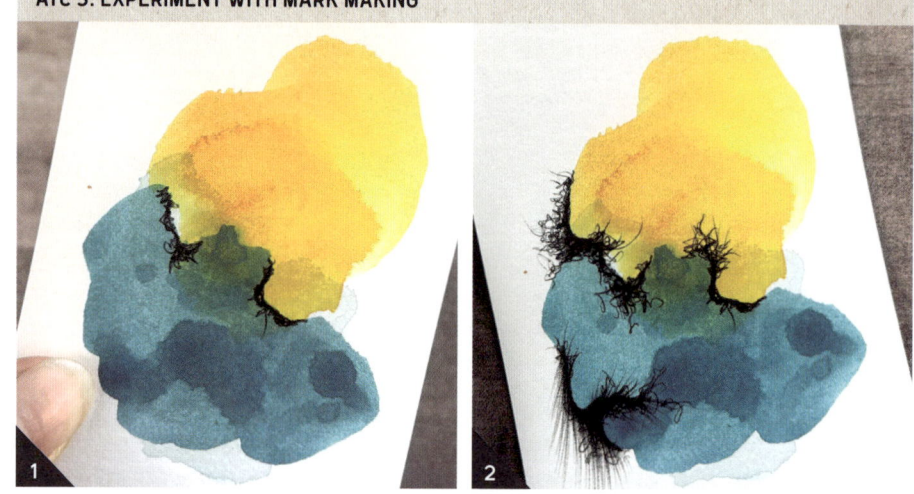

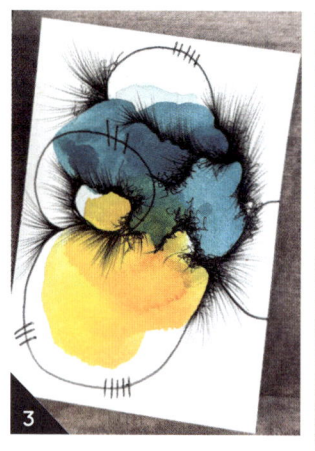

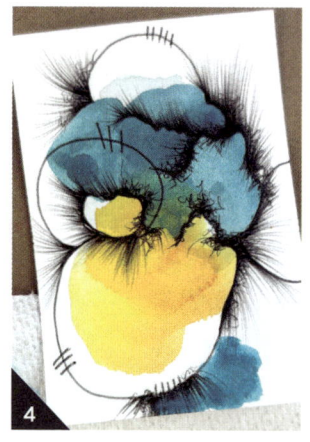

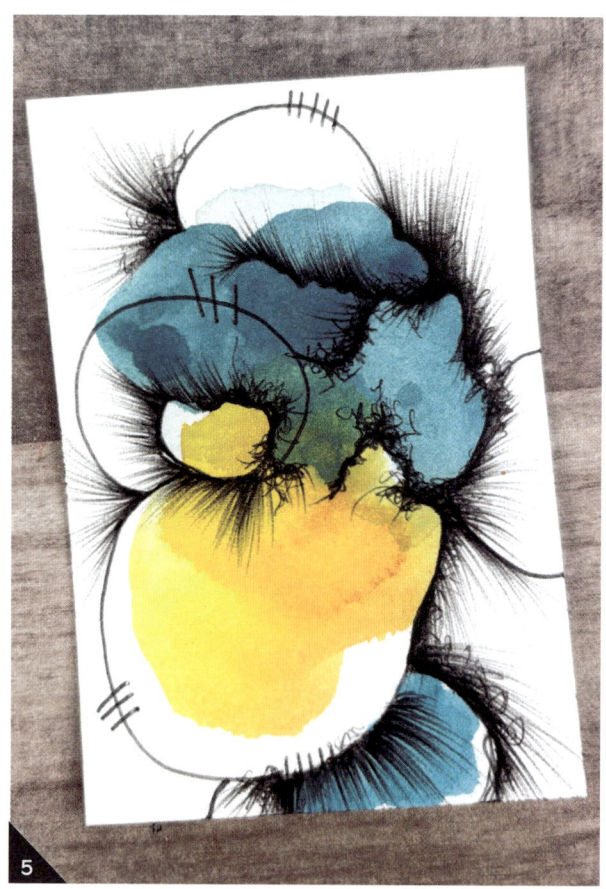

## ATC 3: Experiment with mark making

1. Use a scribble to respond to the existing ink forms. Make the pen as minimal or maximal as you like.

2. Just like in the last ATC, use the scribble to accentuate painted ink forms by working around them.

3. Bring the pen into the negative space. Use any type or mark you like. I made rounded, arching shapes and short hatches to add interest to the white space.

4. If your marks bring elements of the drawing off the edge of the ATC, think about touching at least three sides of the format. Here, I went back in with some aqua ink at the bottom edge. This made the composition less centrally focused and brought some visual weight to the bottom.

5. Complete your drawing by checking all areas are in harmony. If not, add some more marks with the pen. I wanted to make the newly painted section appear as if it was always there, so I added more marks to that area.

### TOP TIP

With all abstract drawing, you may want to play around with orientation. What side looks better as the top? Will it be vertical or horizontal? It's entirely up to you.

# MIXED MEDIA: WATERCOLOR

As ballpoint pens are waterproof, watercolor is a great way to add color to your drawings. I prefer to use watercolor paint after I've done the pen drawing, but pen can be added on top of a dry watercolor painting. In this exercise, I share a simple technique to build an elegant, organic abstract drawing that we'll enhance with watercolor.

## YOU WILL NEED

- 8 x 11in (20 x 28cm) mixed media paper or hot press watercolor paper
- Medium- or fine-point pen in a dark color
- Low-tack masking tape
- Selection of watercolor paints
- Soft watercolor brushes
- Paint palette
- Jar of water
- Paper towel

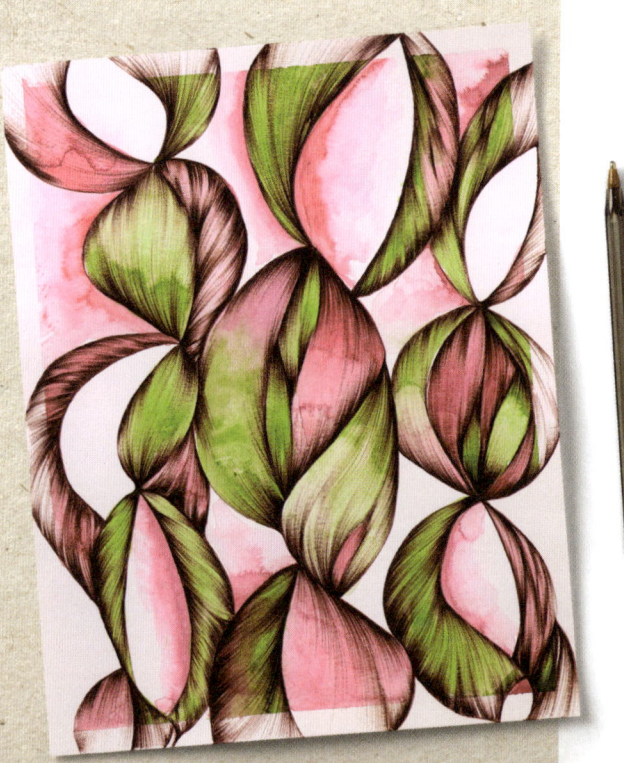

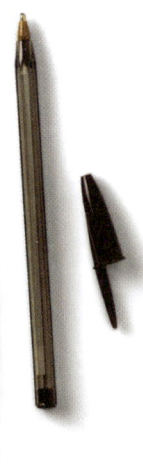

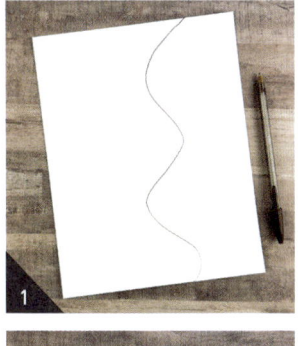
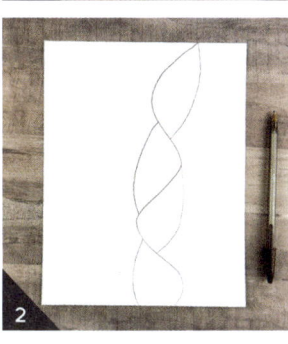
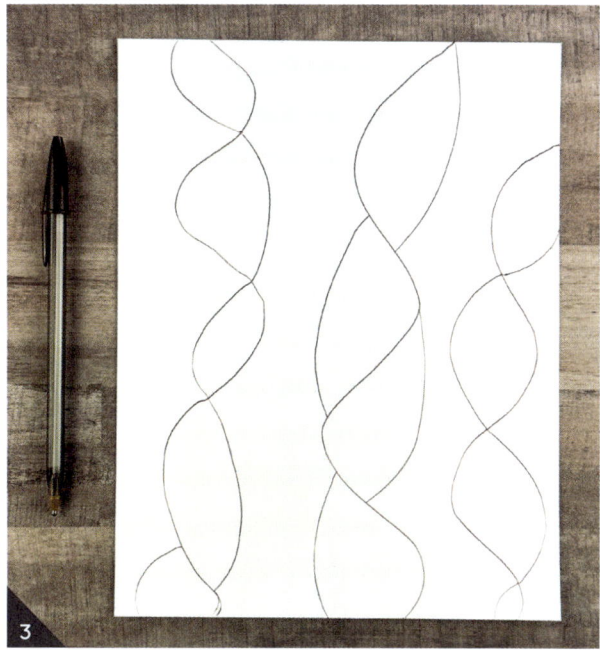

1. Using the pen, draw a wavy line from the top to the bottom of the page. Position this line off-center, so the spaces created are unequal in size.

2. Form leaf shapes by closing in the curves on the initial line. Vary the size and width of the leaves.

3. Add a few more curved lines to fill up the page. It's okay if these lines don't span the entire length of the paper. Try to space the curves in these lines differently than the first to create interest and variety. Fill in the curves with leaf shapes, again varying the size.

## TOP TIP

You may want to tape down your paper before starting, using low-tack masking tape. This will create a border for your drawing but does mean the paper is more laborious to turn, if you wish to.

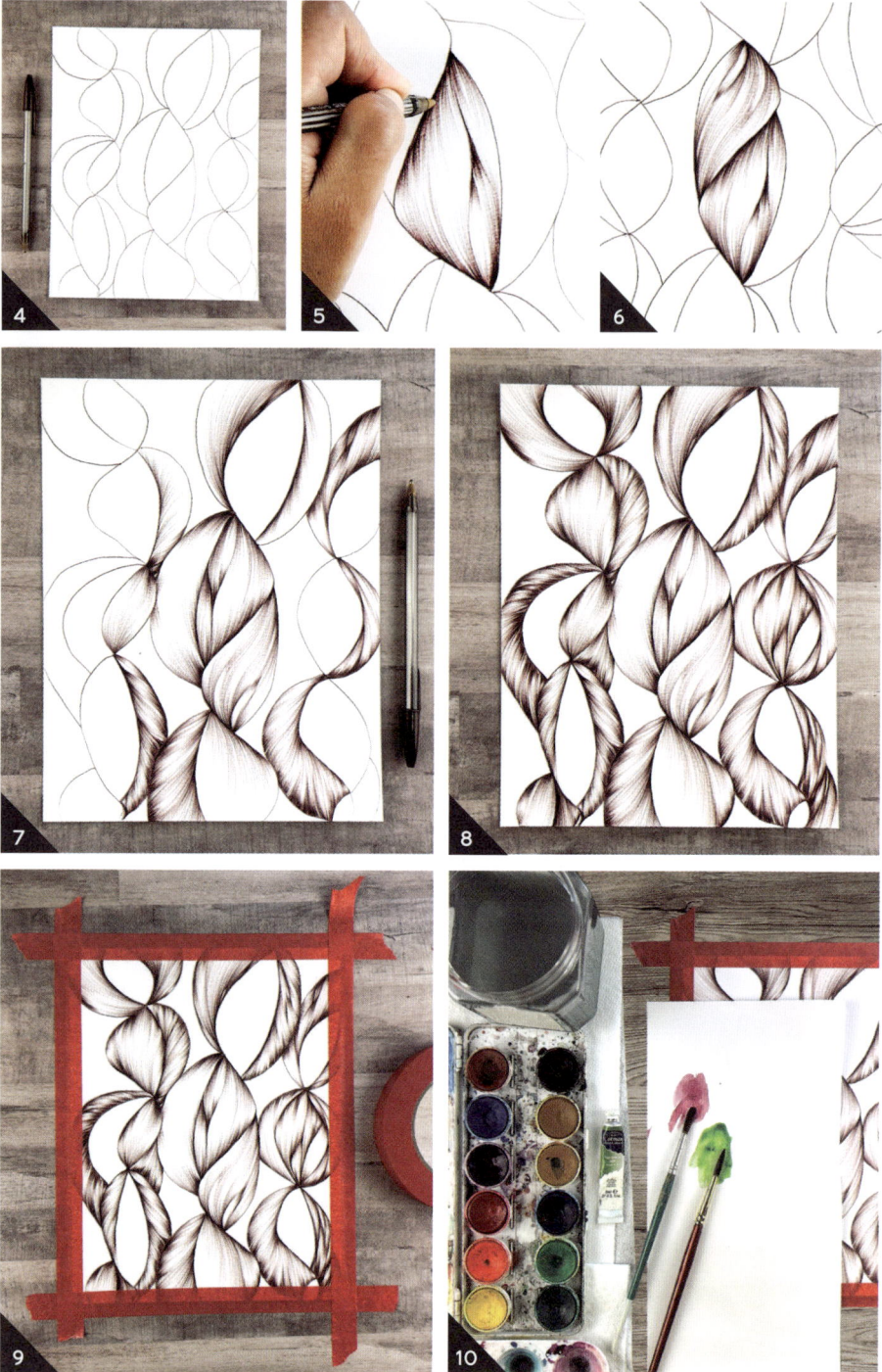

4. Survey the composition as a whole. Is it interesting to you? Are the spaces created varied? I decided that I wanted the three lines of leaves to overlap, so I enlarged some of the leaf shapes. I continued until I had leaf forms going off all four sides of the page and I was satisfied with the positive and negative spaces created.

5. Start shading in the leaves and obscuring the outlines. Go dark up against an edge and lighter towards the middle to give the leaves some roundness. Curve pen strokes with the curve of the leaf. Keep your shading somewhat light, preserving plenty of white paper for the watercolor.

6. Continue to create contrast between leaves with your shading. If an overlapping shape is already dark, keep the edge that touches it light. Divide shapes into smaller transitions if you feel inclined to. Turn your paper often so you are shading in a direction that feels most natural.

7. Apply some of your shading parallel to the edges of the shapes and some perpendicularly. This is another way to create variety and contrast.

8. Continue shading until you have filled all or most of the leaves. You may want to leave some unshaded for variety. I left some of the middle shapes blank to create some interesting negative spaces. Take a look at the drawing as a whole and add additional leaves if needed to make the composition more full or balanced. Play around with orientation. My drawing seemed more interesting upside down.

9. Prepare your work area for watercolor. Unless you've used a very thick paper, there will be some warping when the watercolor is added. To combat this, tape the edges of the paper to your work space with low-tack masking tape prior to painting. Be sure to test the tape to make sure it won't rip the paper when it gets wet.

10. Mix up a palette of two to three watercolors that will complement the color of the pen drawing. I used brown pen, which is a neutral, so I could work with any color scheme. I decided to use a complementary color scheme of yellow-green and red-violet.

11. Start painting anywhere that feels good to you. Use flat values or create transitions by adding more water to the paint to make it fade. Paint the background, the foreground, or both. Painting small areas at a time will prevent the paper from warping too much. Add enough water to the paint so that it flows smoothly and is transparent enough that the pen will show through.

12. If you want to prevent the colors from blending into one another, paint one color at a time and wait until it is dry to paint adjacent shapes. If you want to embrace the unpredictability of watercolor, paint different colors at the same time. I did a little of both. While the paint is still wet, you can use a little piece of paper towel to blot unappealing areas. If you work quickly, you'll be able to remove much of the paint. You can also use this technique to create texture in your painting.

13. Continue to paint until there is a balance of each color around the composition. If the paint dries too lightly for your liking, add another layer of paint. If you like what you see, stop there and admire your work!

14. If the white background feels too stark, add some color to it. This will also cover up places where you may have colored outside of the lines. With some strong paint (just a little water), paint along the edge of a leaf shape. Clean your brush and apply water to the wet paint edge. Let the paint and water do their thing and create an interesting texture. Blot with a paper towel for added texture. I ended up using only the red-violet color in the background, and did leave some spaces unpainted.

15. Let the paint dry thoroughly before removing the tape. If needed, work back in with a pen to enhance the darks and cover up any wavy painted edges. Cut off the unpainted edges or leave them. If you choose to mat (mount) your finished piece, it's helpful to have that edge for mounting.

## TOP TIP

Watercolor by nature can be difficult to control, but that's also part of its charm. Relax and let the water flow where it will. You'll end up with some beautiful textures and blooms of color.

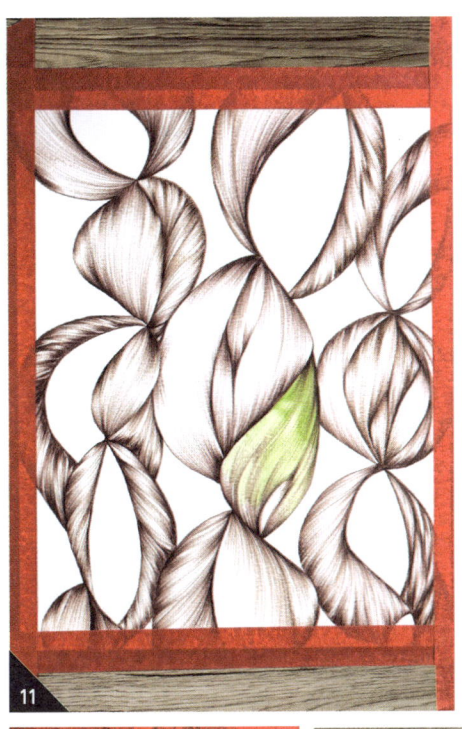

11

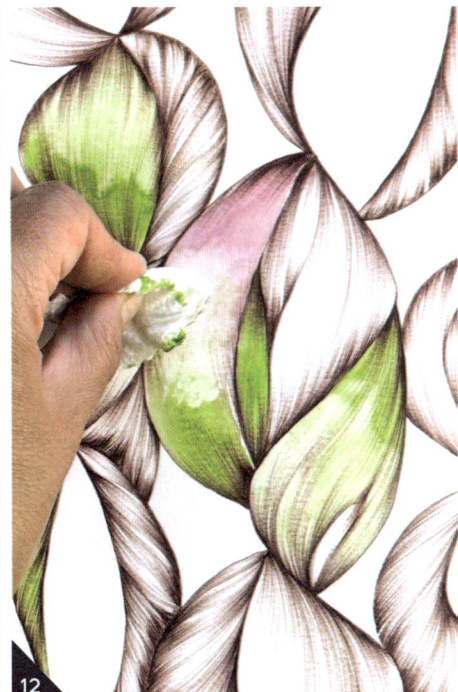

12

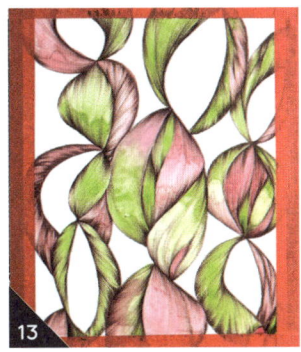

13

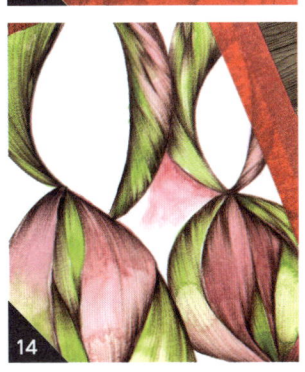

14

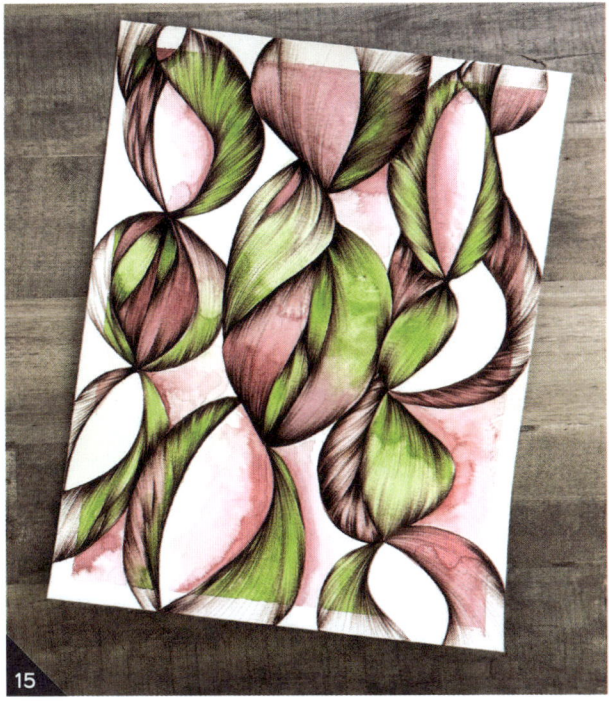

15

# CHAPTER 3
# TEXTURE AND PATTERN

I am a sucker for pattern and texture in a drawing. They add interest and detail, and can be soothing or even meditative to create. A pattern is created by repeating a line, shape, or mark (think stripes or polka dots). Texture has to do with the way something feels (think fur or tree bark). A ballpoint is an excellent tool for the repetitive mark making necessary to form both textures and patterns. In this section, you'll work to develop your own signature mark-making techniques. Approach these as exercises and studies, and not finished drawings, as this will free your hand. I also share some tips and tricks for drawing hair, feathers, and wood grain.

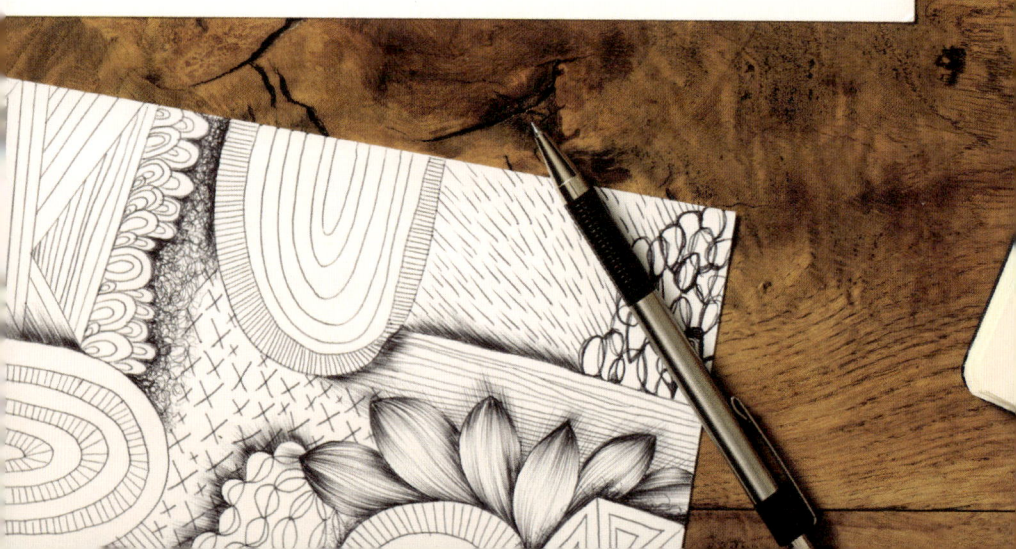

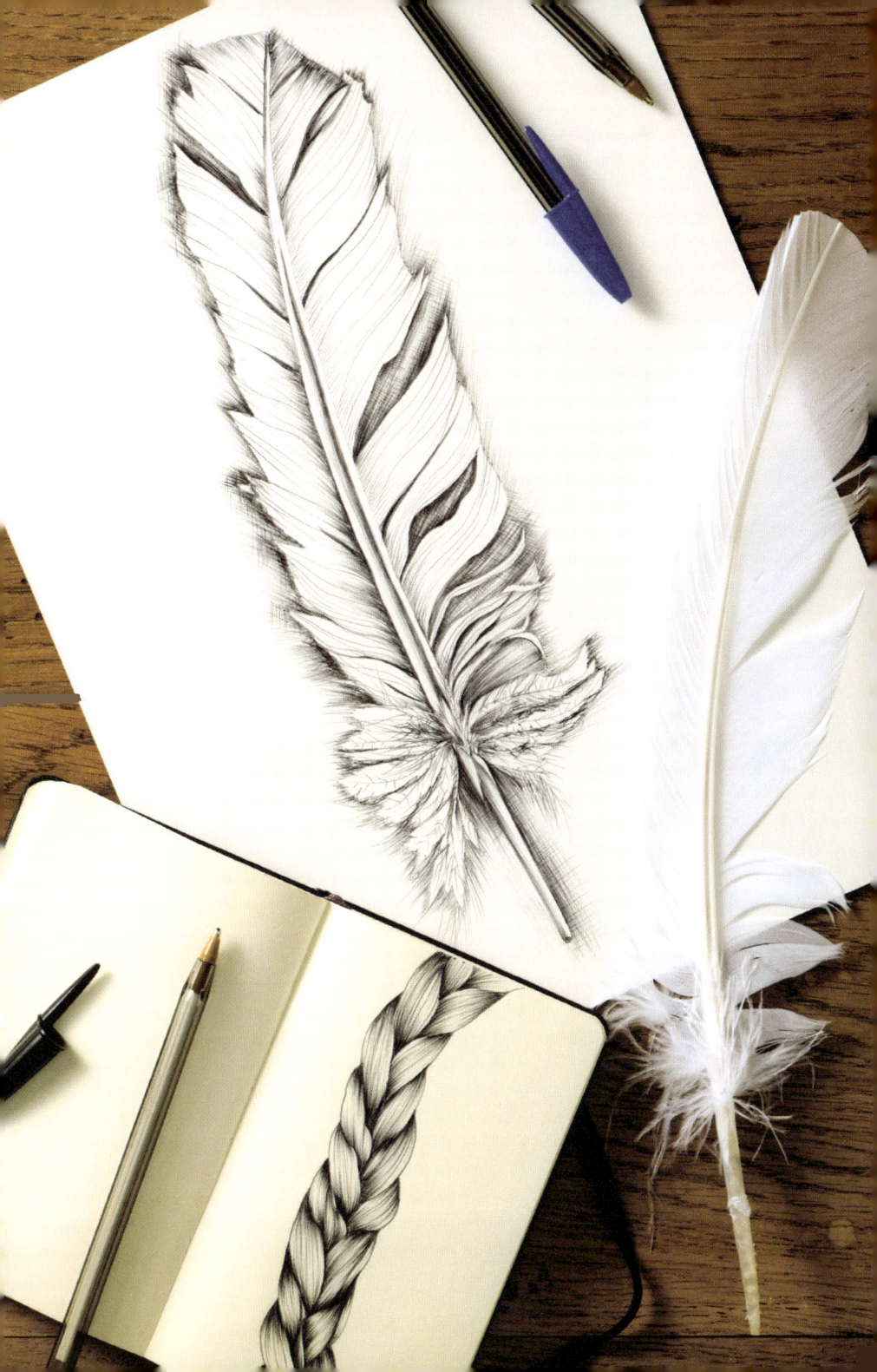

# FEATHERS

Birds were a major focus of my work for
many years, so I've gotten pretty good
at drawing feathers. For this exercise, try
to draw a feather from life, if possible.
Seeing the feather up close will help you
understand its structure. As the feather is
white, we'll be drawing the negative space
and shadows more than the feather itself.

## YOU WILL NEED

- Sketchbook or
  smooth paper
- Fine-point pen in
  a dark color
- Feather (or a
  photo of one)

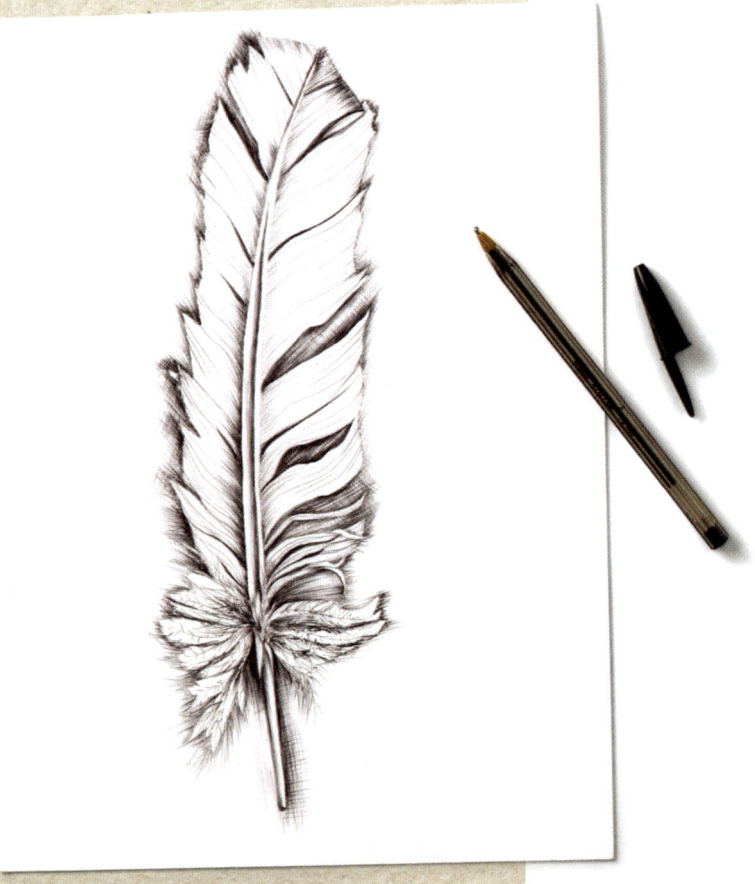

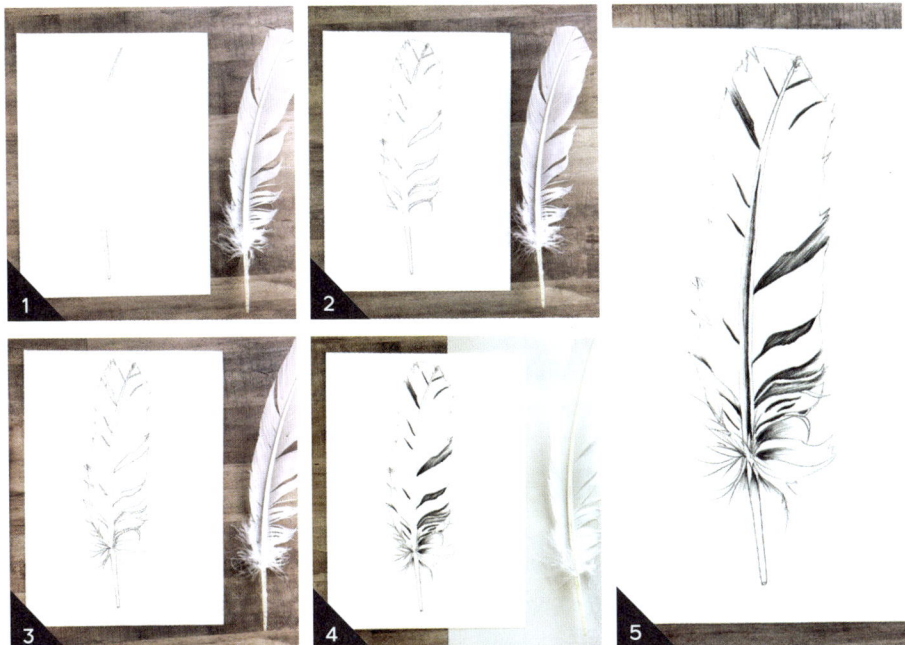

1. Start by drawing the tube-shaped rachis (the middle of the feather) and the quill (the bottom part of the feather). Notice its curve and how it thins at the ends. I left a little space where the fluffy afterfeathers cover the quill.

2. Draw in the dark negative spaces to mark the splits in the feather and lightly sketch the outer edges of the vane (the flat part of the feather). Keep it loose and light and don't worry about recording every detail.

3. Sketch in the location and direction of the fluffy feathers at the bottom of the vane with some fine lines.

4. Add in the shadows. Shade in the negative spaces using strokes that go in the same direction as the vane. Shade in the smaller spaces entirely and in the larger breaks, create transitions. Go darkest right up against the edge and fade as you get farther away.

5. Add shading to the rachis to show the hollow in the middle.

## TOP TIP

Place your feather on a piece of white paper so that the shadows are more visible.

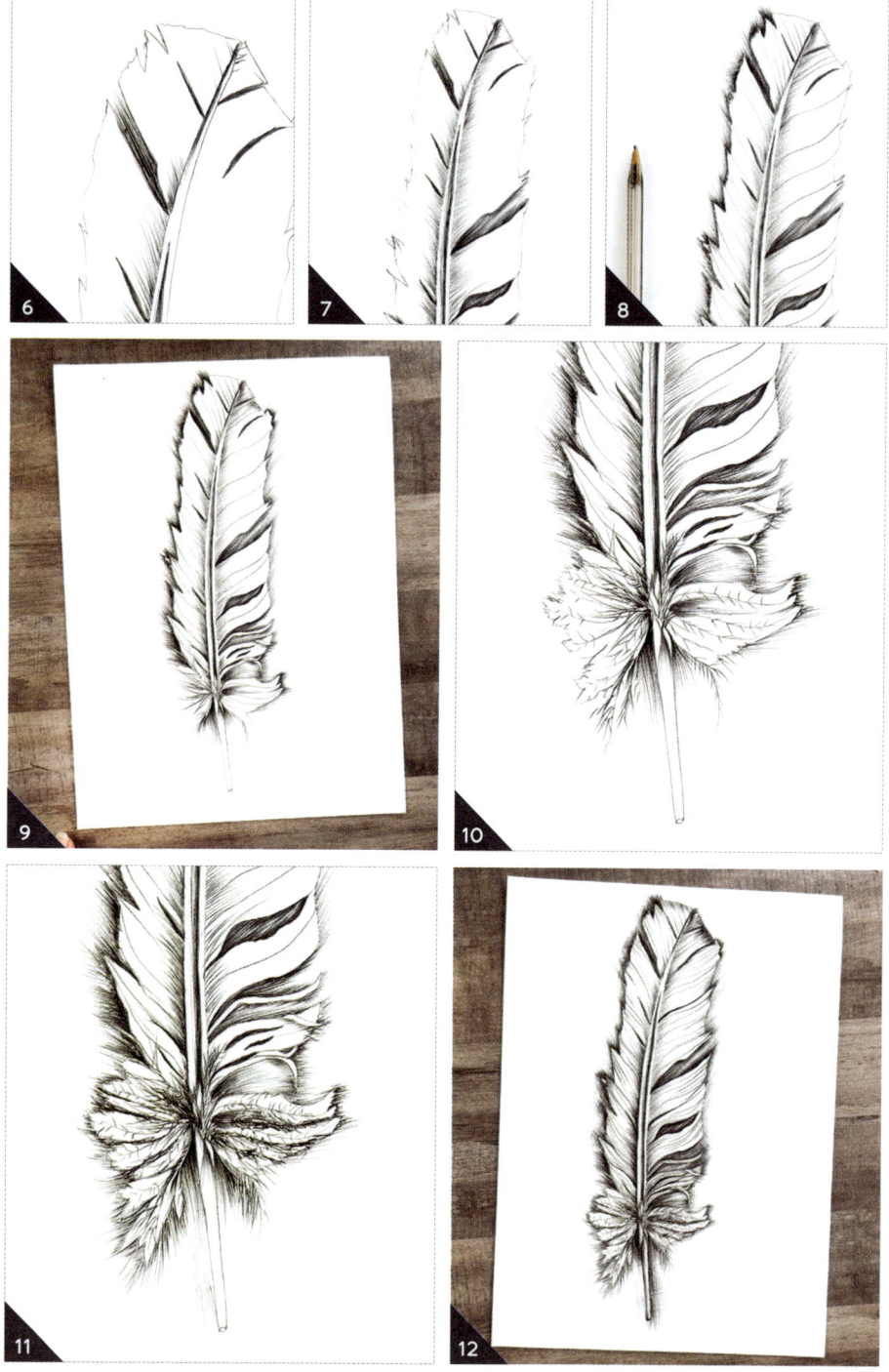

6. To form the light edge on the left of the rachis, use fine lines to draw the vanes that are in the shadow on the left side of the rachis. Go slowly and flick your wrist at the end of your stroke so that it ends in a very fine point. Notice how the shadows shift onto the left side of the rachis itself towards the top.

7. Add a bit of shading to the right side of the rachis. Keep it lighter than the left side. The angle of the vanes on this side will probably be slightly different, so try to reflect that with your shading.

8. Create the shadows that are cast onto the table by the edges of the feather. Usually, the shadow will be darker on one side than the other. You could cross-hatch or scribble so that the shadow contrasts with the feather itself. If you decide to shade smoothly, consider switching to a wide-point pen. Notice how the edge is made up of countless tiny vanes, so embrace imperfection and let it be jagged.

9. Shade the other side of the feather, keeping it lighter overall than the opposite side. If the feather itself is darker than the background, don't shade this part of background, such as the top right of the feather.

10. Look closely at the fluffy feathers at the bottom of the vane (the afterfeathers). Notice the delicate v-shapes on each little strand and add some of those in. Keep it light overall. You'll only need to draw a few to get the point across.

11. Make a light outline around the afterfeathers. Instead of drawing this outline right up against the feather shapes, leave a little white space. Shade away from the outline. Work back into the afterfeathers with some darks to illustrate the layers of feathers on top of one another. I used a quick, scribbly mark.

12. Now it's time to polish. Squint at the feather and at your drawing, so that you see only value. Notice areas that could go darker and start there, such as on the left edge of the rachis. Switch back to a fine-point pen if that's helpful. I added some cross-hatching to the cast shadow areas around the feather to add some interest and variety. Continue cleaning up any harsh edges with some soft shading.

## TOP TIP

Don't get bogged down in detail or perfection. No one will look at your drawing next to the source material. If it differs from the actual feather, that's absolutely fine. Mine sure does!

# BRAIDS

I've been told time and time again that my drawings resemble hair and braids. Though I draw those shapes from memory, if it's not something you've drawn before, it's good to work from a photo or a model at first. In this exercise, I'm working from a braided water hyacinth place mat, but the same technique could be applied to braided hair.

## YOU WILL NEED

- Sketchbook or smooth paper
- Fine-point pen in a dark color
- Something with a braided texture or a photo of braided hair
- Tape (optional)

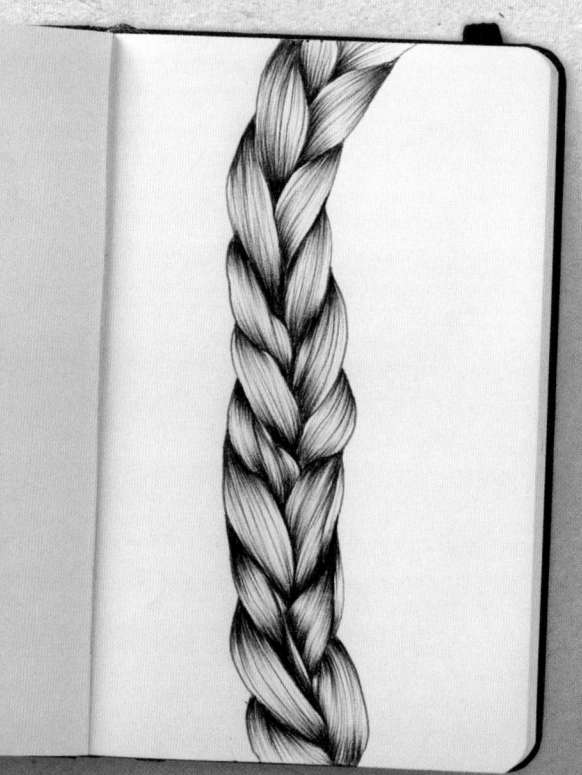

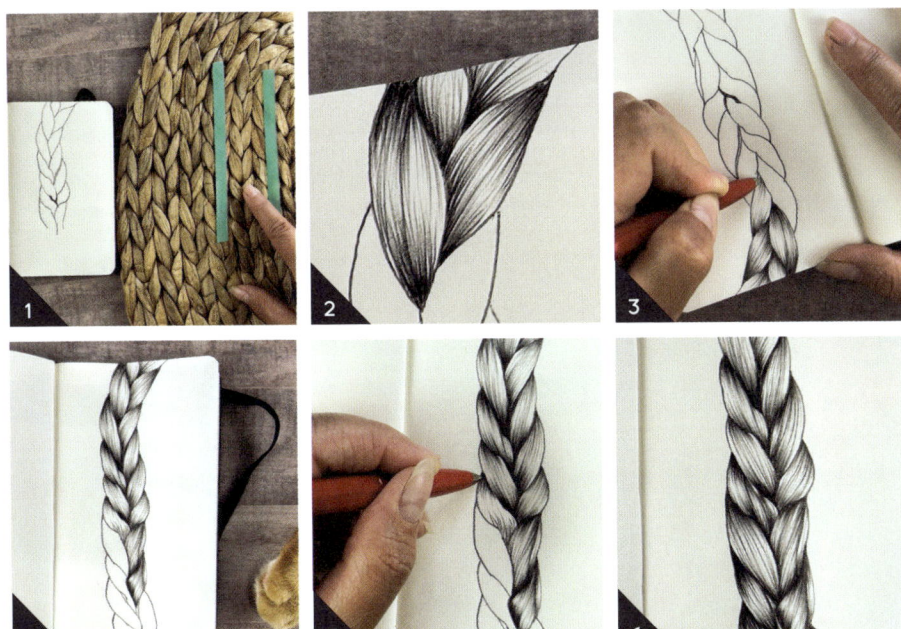

1. If you want some guidance, outline the section that you are drawing with tape. Now, draw the outline of each piece of the braid. Notice how each piece weaves under and over the other. Don't aim for perfection, just draw what you see without judgment.

2. Start with shading a shape at the top of the braid with your pen, showing how it weaves underneath another shape. Using long, flowing lines and a light touch, shade in the direction the hair or fiber runs in the braid. Go dark on the end that weaves underneath and fade to light as it emerges.

3. If it's helpful, turn your sketchbook or paper so that you're shading in a direction that's most natural. I prefer to shade in a downward direction, so I turn my drawing each time I shade a dark end.

4. Continue working your way down the braid, obscuring the outlines with shading. Create contrast between the overlapping shapes by keeping light edges on shapes that are on top and going darker on those that are underneath. Allow your pets to help, if they want!

5. So that the direction of the lines in the transition mimic the source, you can make notes with little lines at both ends of the shape. Then go back in and fully shade the form.

6. Once everything is shaded, add some fine lines to represent individual strands. Only a few are needed around the drawing to get the point across.

# WOOD GRAIN

During my years drawing chairs and room interiors, I've gotten pretty adept at drawing wood grain. It's all about the detail, and developing techniques to describe it on paper with marks and values. Though I like to model my wood grain from life, I modify and simplify the shapes I see as needed.

## YOU WILL NEED

- Sketchbook or smooth paper
- Fine-point pens in black, brown, and orange
- Piece of wood or a photo of one

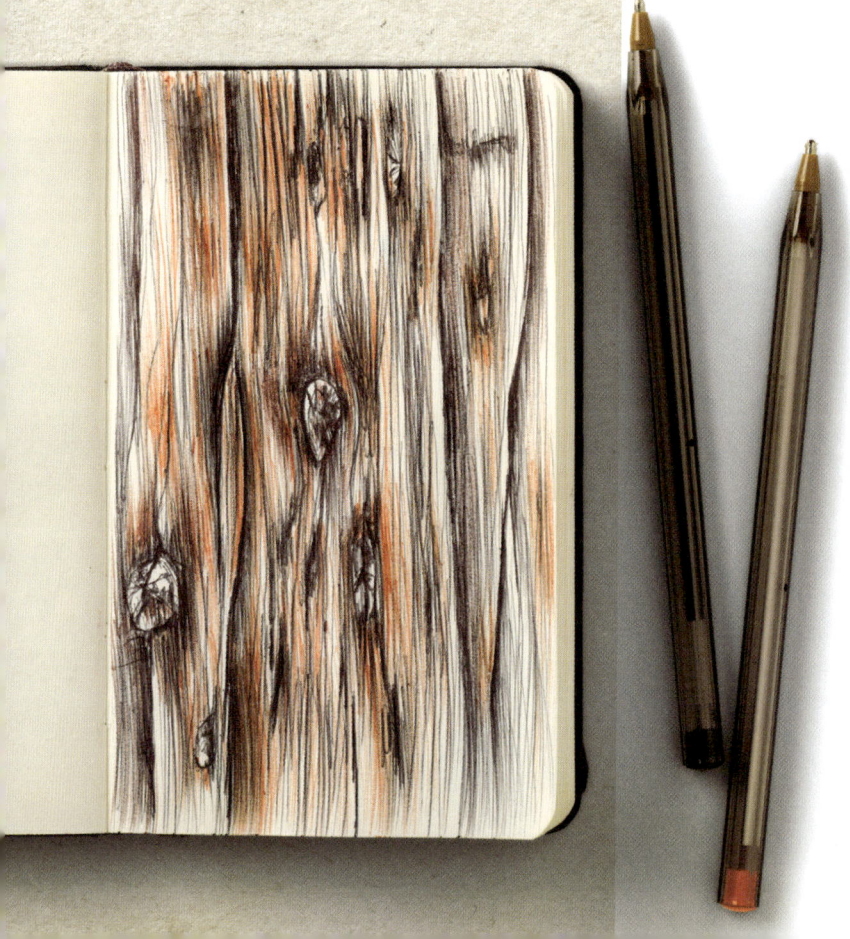

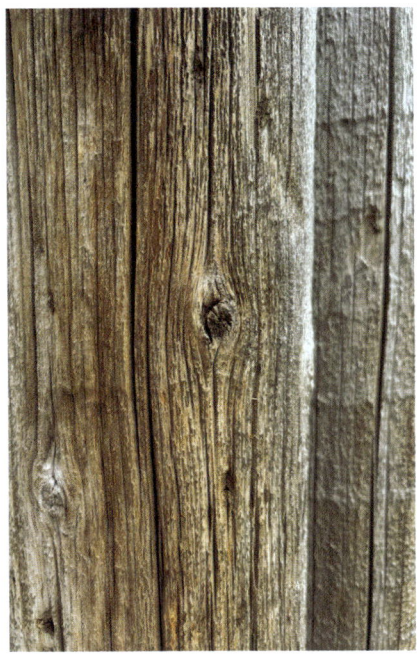
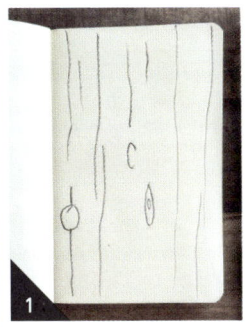
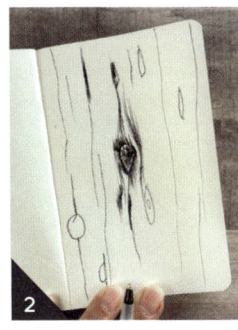
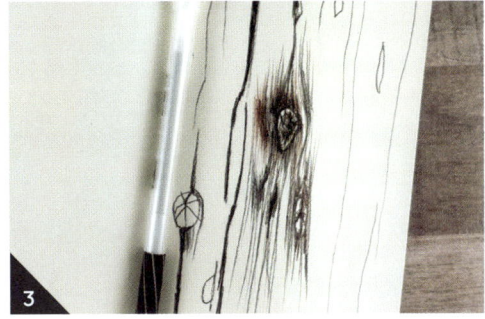

1. With a black pen, use a combination of shapes and lines to draw the darkest areas in the wood. Don't feel compelled to draw everything you see, but just try to describe the main lines, shapes, and edges.

2. Choose a dark knot as a starting point for the shading. Make marks that mimic and describe the values and texture of the knot. Try a combination of scribbles, short hatches, and fine lines.

3. Photorealism is not the goal. Instead, work to loosely mimic what you see. I added in the brown as a test. Then, I continued on with the black.

## TOP TIP

With so much detail, drawing wood can be intimidating. The key is to simplify and to look for patterns. Instead of trying to draw everything you see, focus on a small area and draw it with simple lines. Once you've got the hang of it, repeat the pattern to fill the space.

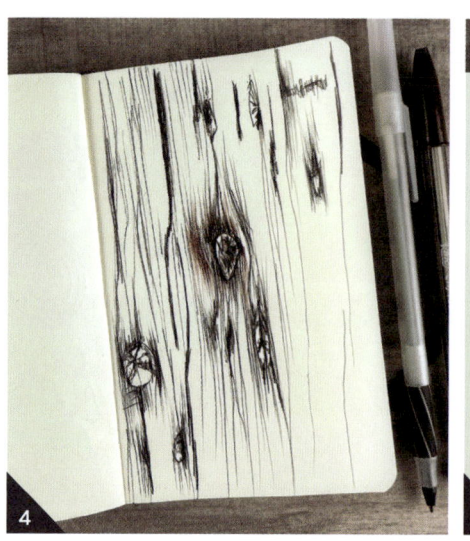

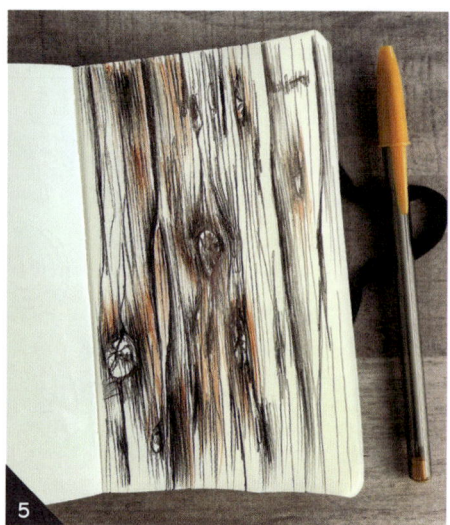

4

5

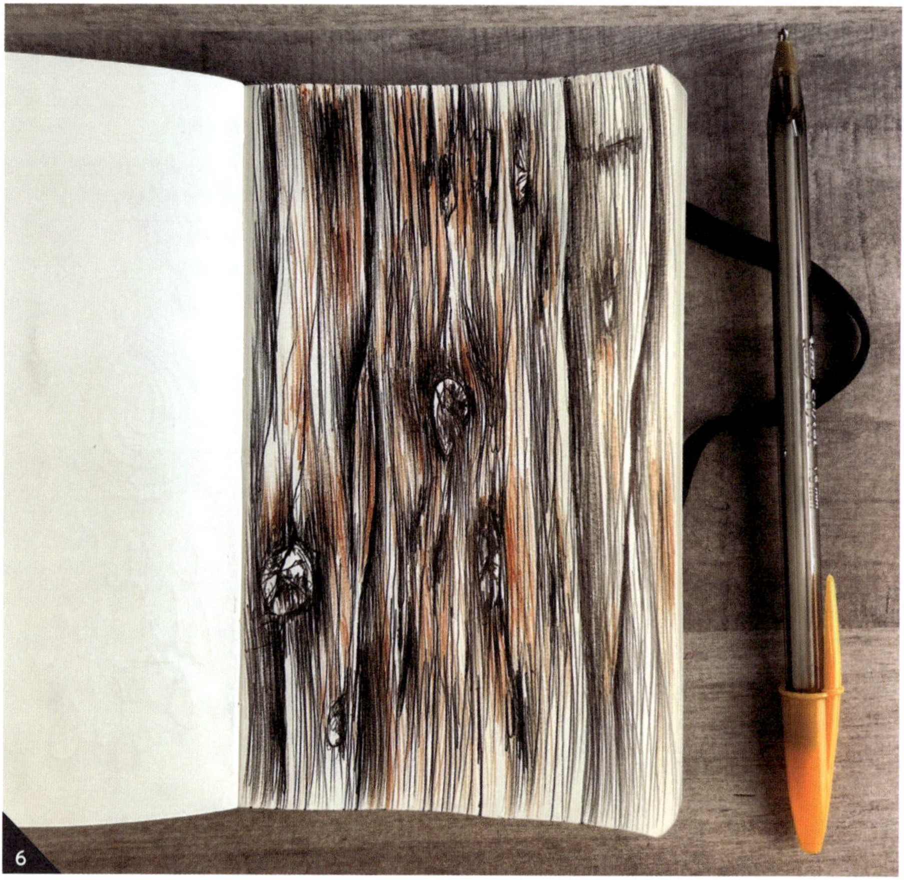

6

4. Choose another nearby knot or dark spot and add shading there. Connect the shading and mark making to the initial knot. Repeat until you've added darks to all of the knots. Then, fill in the space with more fine, long lines to indicate the grain. Be confident and don't worry about making a mistake.

5. Squint at your source photo and notice what areas stand out more than the rest. Start working in the brown and/ or orange into those areas. Vary the concentration of color you add so that everything doesn't start to look the same.

6. Keep adding color and line work until you're happy with it. Remember, photorealism doesn't need to be the end goal. Aim to capture the overall texture and feeling of the wood.

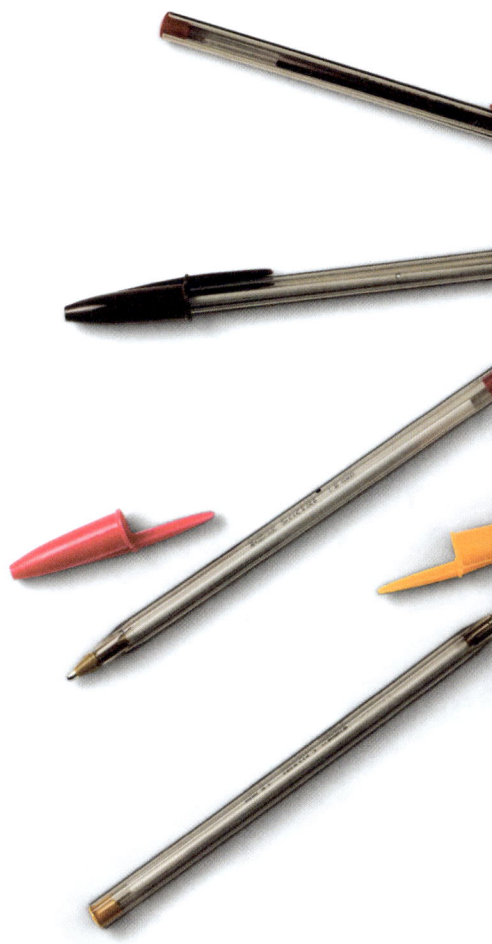

# SIGNATURE MARKS

Some of my favorite mark-making techniques have come to me when I allowed myself the freedom to experiment and play with no expectation. For this exercise, don't worry about making a finished product, just make marks and have fun! If you're a doodler, like I am, start with the shapes or motifs that often show up in your doodles. If you're not a doodler, start with a stripe or another basic shape like a circle, square, or triangle.

## YOU WILL NEED

- Sketchbook or copy paper in any size
- Fine-point pen in any color
- Pencil
- Ruler (optional)

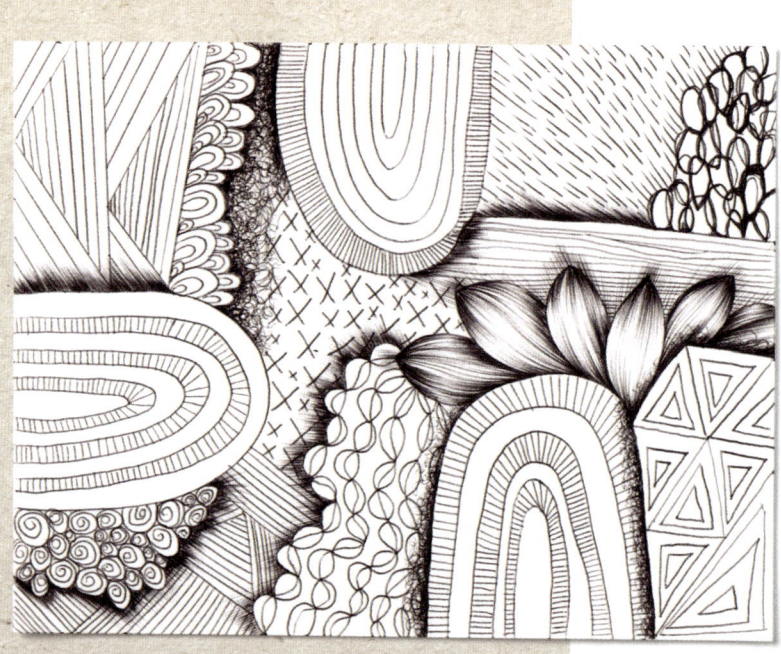
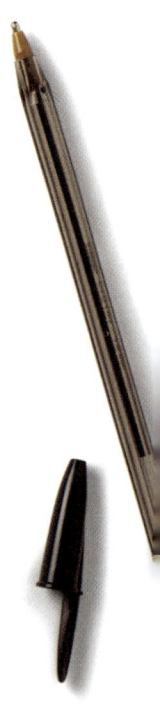

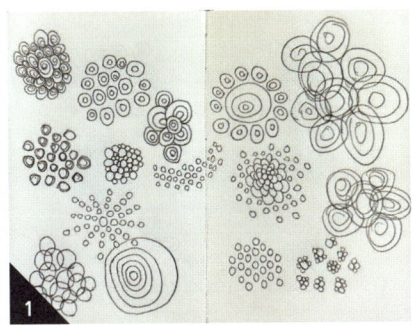

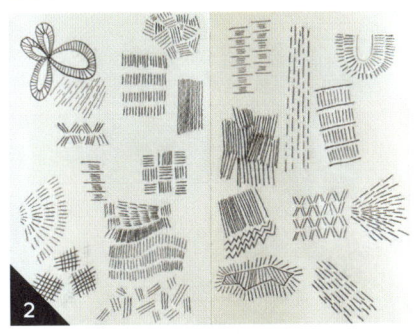

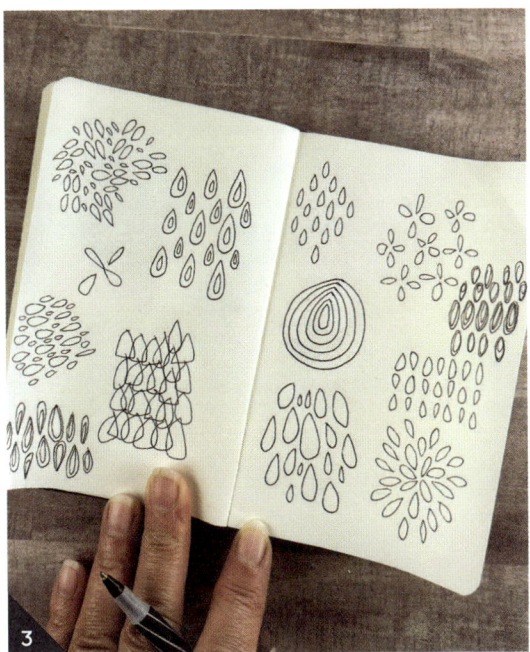

1. On a sketchbook page or blank piece of paper, come up with as many different motifs as you can using one shape. Play with both orderly and random patterns, and experiment with the scale and spacing of the shapes. What happens when the shapes overlap or are spaced evenly?

2. Try giving yourself some parameters. For instance, only use short, straight lines. This forces you to get creative while also making it easier to get started. Ideas will often lead to more ideas. Not all of them will be good, but the more you play, the easier the ideas come.

3. Repeat this exercise with a few other shapes. With each pattern, strive for experimentation and not perfection. Fill as many sheets or pages as you like. Relax and play.

## TOP TIP

Work on copy paper or in a sketchbook, so there's less pressure and you won't worry about wasting paper.

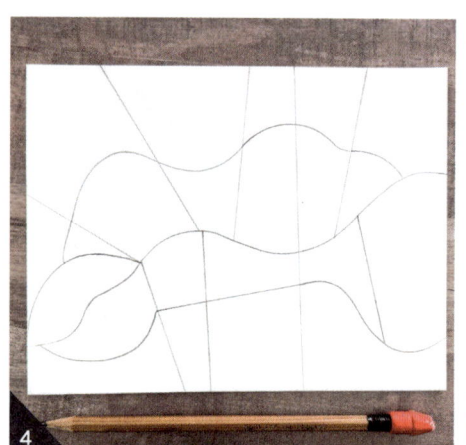

4

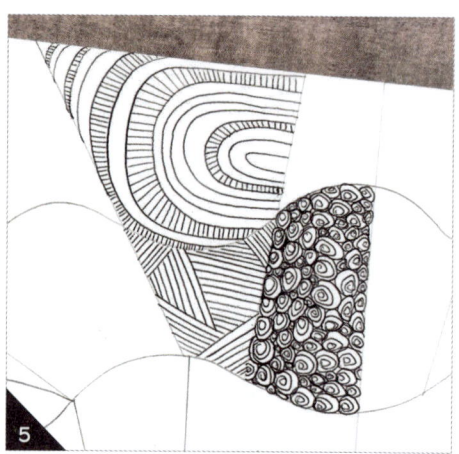

5

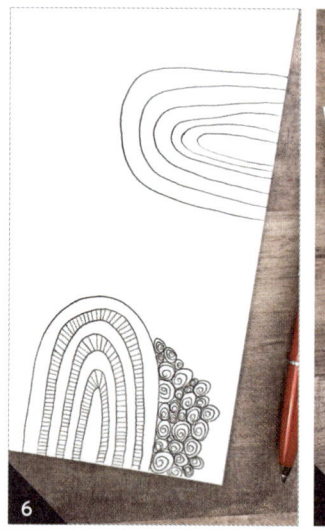

6

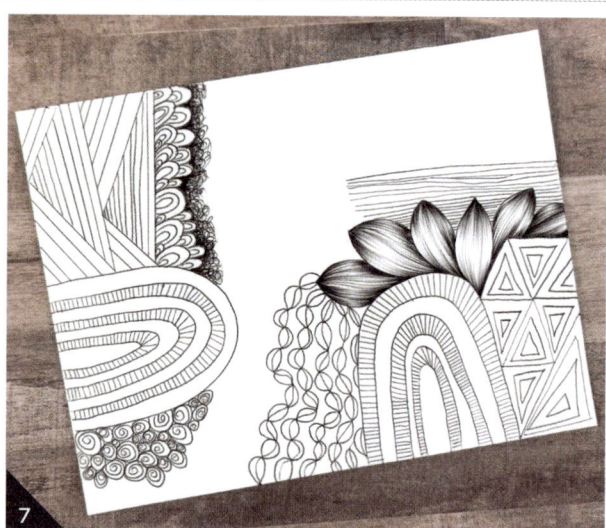

7

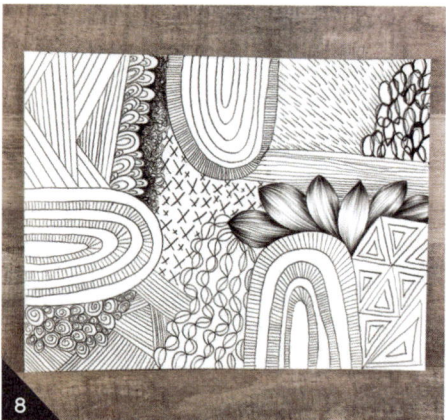

8

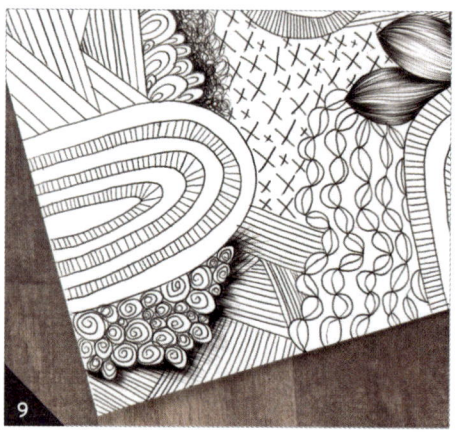

9

4. On a sketchbook page or a piece of smooth paper, create a pattern sample. Use a pencil to divide your format into multiple sections. Draw straight lines, curved lines, or both, varying the size of the spaces created. Draw lightly, so the lines can be erased or covered easily with ink.

5. Choose some of your favorite patterns and add them to the spaces with pen. Try to create contrast between neighboring shapes by placing large patterns next to small ones, and darker patterns next to lighter ones. Don't worry about making mistakes, just work on honing your visual language.

6. Alternatively, you can jump right into the drawing without dividing the space, which is what I did, while still trying to create contrast.

7. As you work, experiment with combining elements of different patterns together to make new patterns. If new pattern ideas pop up, use them! If it's helpful, use a ruler to draw straight edged patterns. Repeat patterns if you like or make every pattern different. Vary the amount of space that each pattern takes up to add interest.

8. Once you've filled the page with patterns, feel free to be done and admire your work!

9. If you feel like continuing on, think about how you can create greater contrast between neighboring shapes with some shading. Create cast shadows of sorts with a shading technique of your choice, such as scribble shading or some hatching.

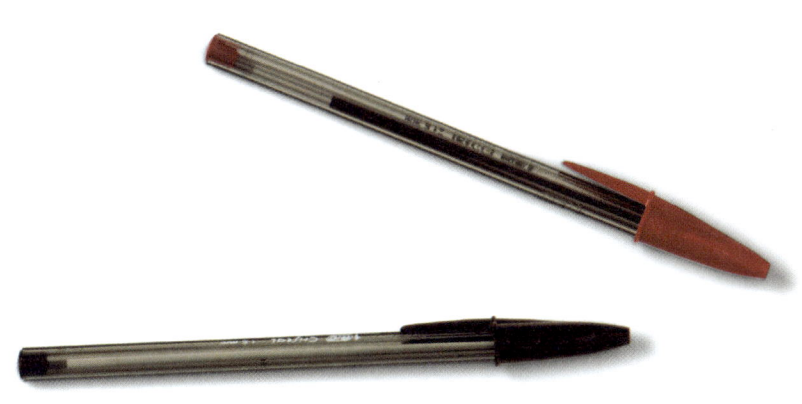

# CHAPTER 4
# THEMES

Though my recent work is mainly abstract,
I have explored many other subjects over
the years. In this chapter, I'll share projects
featuring some of my favorite subject matter
and I'll introduce you to some new techniques
along the way. A photo reference was
used in all the projects, but many of these
subjects could also be drawn from life.

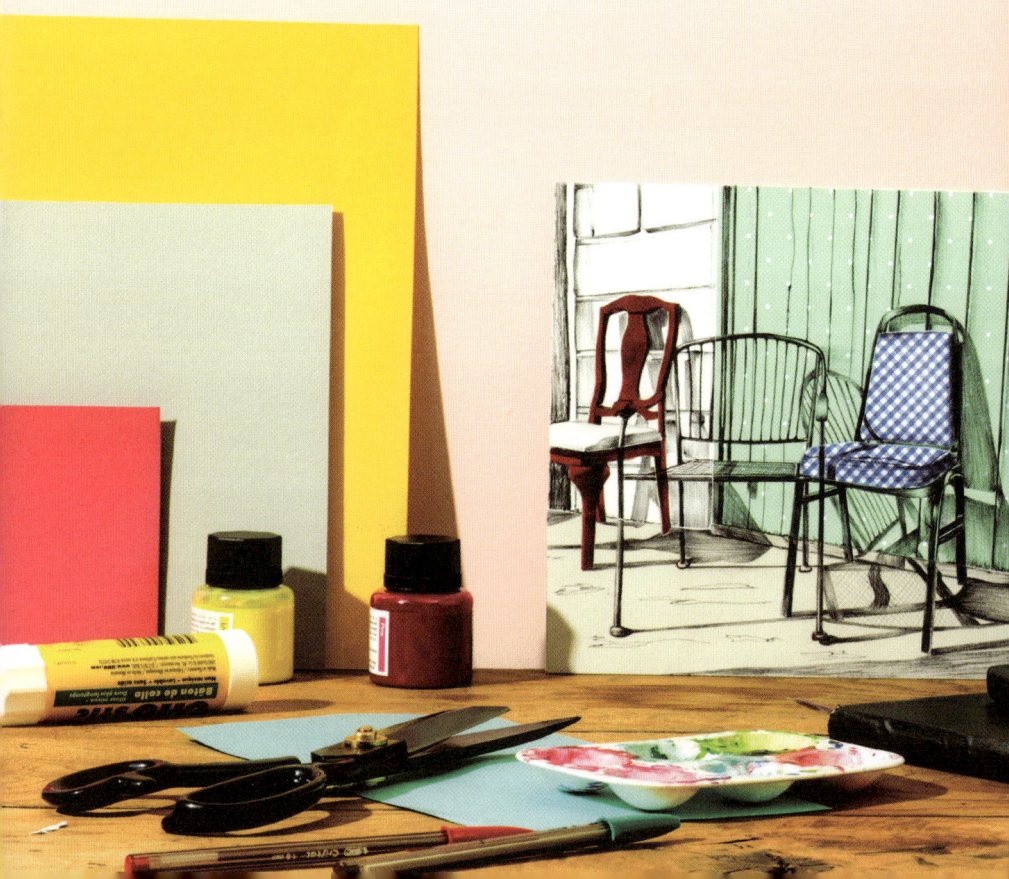

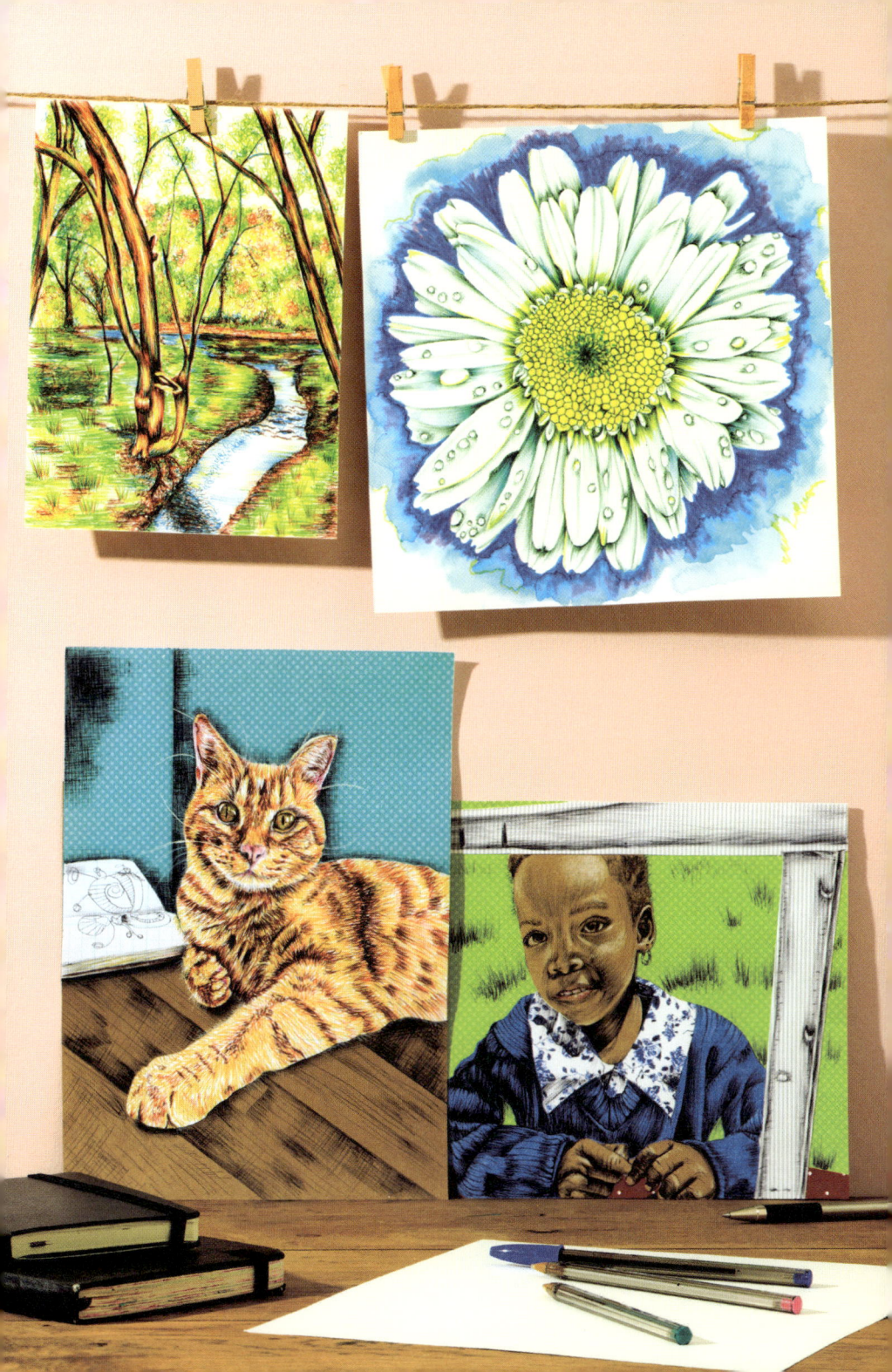

# ANIMALS

Sir Richard, my two-year-old orange cat, is my shadow and studio supervisor. He's been at my feet or right up on my drawing table for nearly every minute I've worked on this book, so it seems fitting that he makes an appearance. In this drawing, I'll use collage paper to add color to the background and pens to render Sir Richard lounging on top of my drawing table in a 7½ x 10in (19 x 25.5cm) sized image.

## YOU WILL NEED

- Smooth white paper or graph paper
- Tracing paper or carbon paper
- Image of a cat
- Low-tack masking tape
- Fine-point pens in a variety of colors such as black, gold, green, pink, orange, and brown
- Selection of colored and/ or patterned paper
- Craft knife or scissors
- Double-sided mounting film or glue stick
- Pencil
- Ruler
- White gel pen

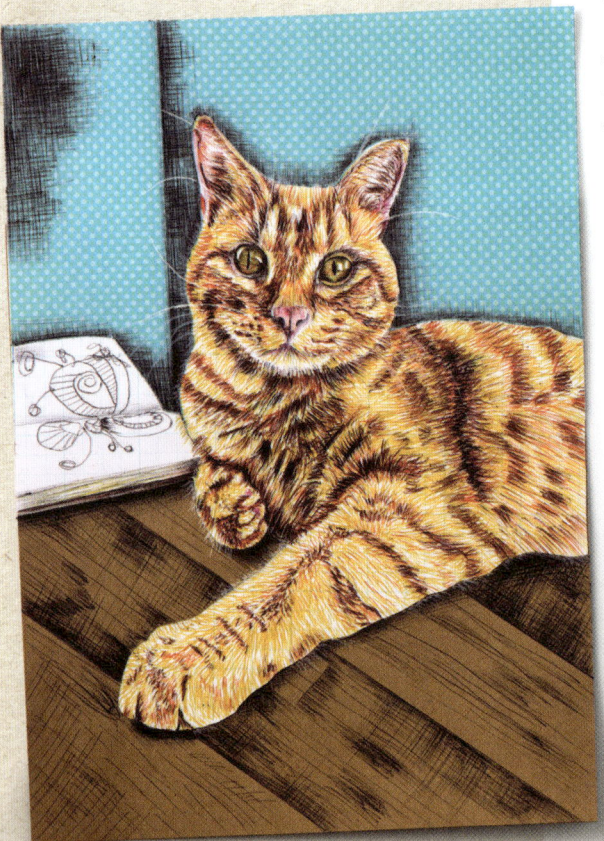

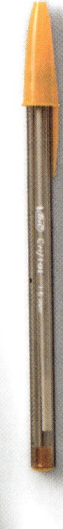

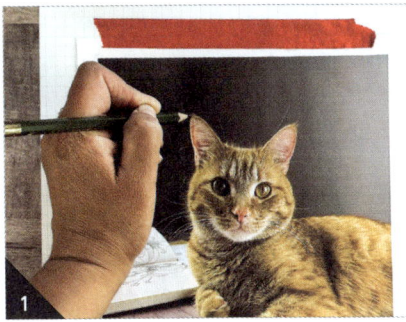
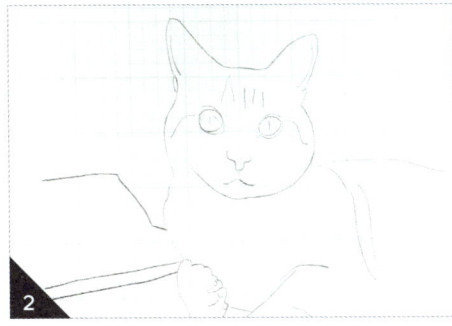

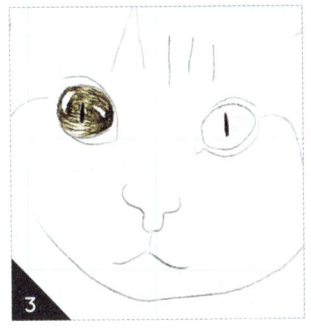
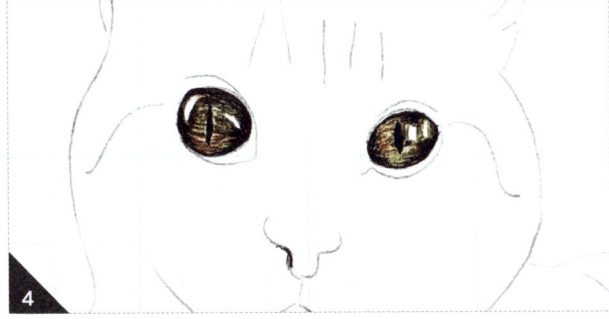

1. Using some tape, secure the photo to a white sheet of paper that will serve as the background for the cat drawing. I used graph paper to add some interest, but plain white paper works just as well. With some carbon paper sandwiched in between, lightly trace over the major shapes of the cat in pencil, transferring those lines onto the graph paper. This can also be done with tracing paper or even a bright window.

2. Don't worry about the whiskers or bits of fur that protrude from the body of the cat at this point.

3. Using a fine-point black pen, shade in the sliver of the pupil. Using a gold (if available) or even a green, shade the iris, working with slightly rounded strokes to show the roundness of the eye. Leave some white space for the reflection in the eye. There is a bit of orange in the irises, so lightly add that in, blending the orange into the gold.

4. With a black pen, outline the iris and then add the darkest shadows to the irises.

## TOP TIP

Zoom in on the eyes if you've got a digital version of the source photo. Even if you don't include it all, it's helpful to see and understand the structures up close.

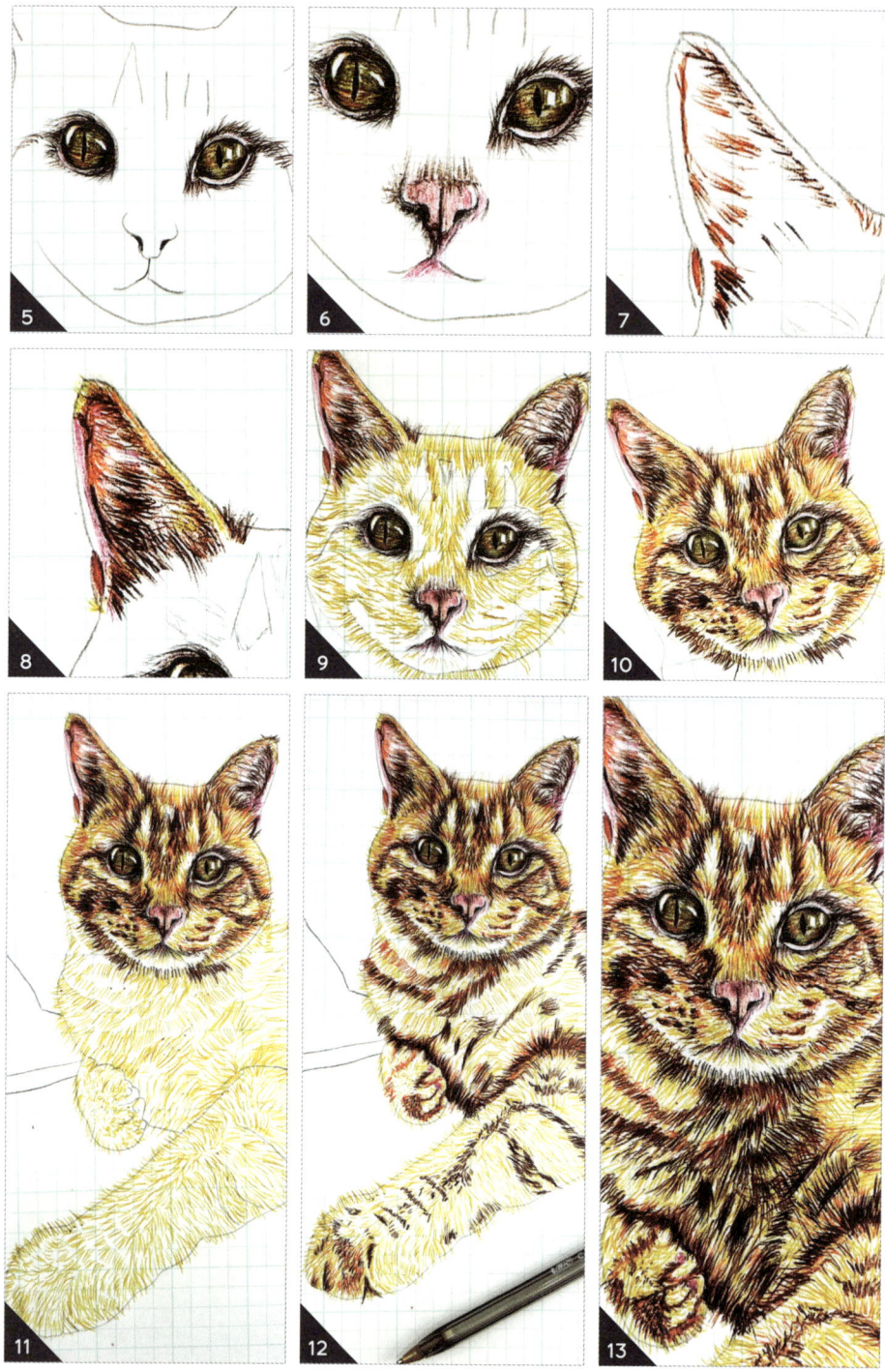

5. Using brown and/or black, shade the inner corners of the eyes and the darks of the eyelids. Notice the pink of the eyelid around the eye. You can use some pink there or keep it white and shade around it with fine brown or black lines in the direction of the fur growth.

6. Moving onto the nose, add the shadows of the nostrils. Use a fine-point pen to make the sharp edge of the nostril and then shade away from it, transitioning from dark to light. Using a bit of pink, orange, and brown, use a light touch to add color to the nose. Pay attention to the edges and notice which are light and which are dark. Add a bit of pink to denote the tiny sliver of Richard's top lip that is visible. With a light touch and a fine-point black pen, add some fine lines to create the faint shadow there.

7. Take a close look at the ears and their darks and lights. To create the illusion of the white hairs, shade the darks around the light hairs using fur-like strokes in brown and orange.

8. Use a mix of pink, orange, and yellow to add value to the rest of the ear. Continue to use short fur-like strokes. Leave the outline around the white edge of the ear for now.

9. Make a note of the light areas on the face using pencil, then work around them to add color and value. Start with the lightest color in your palette and use short lines to suggest the fur. Pay attention to the direction that the fur is growing. Don't worry about the whiskers, as these will be added at the end.

10. Repeat the process with your medium and dark values until you've described the major shapes of the face. If you need to, introduce some black into the darkest areas.

11. Now use the same technique for the rest of the body, starting with the light colors.

12. Add your medium colors on top. To achieve realistic-looking fur, make marks in the various directions it lies. Use longer lines on the torso and the shortest lines on the paw.

13. Add the dark color to the fur. Don't worry about the edges or covering the outlines at this point.

14. If you're using a double-sided mounting film to glue the collage elements, apply it to the back of the drawing now. If not, head straight into cutting. Using a craft knife or scissors, carefully cut out the cat. Cut jaggedly where the fur protrudes away from the body. I also shaded and cut out around the sketchbook on the left.

15. Choose some collage elements to serve as the background. Use colors that will complement the color palette of the cat. I chose an aqua paper to add some color to the wall behind Richard and to make his orange fur pop. I also chose a brown craft paper for the tabletop. Lay the drawing on top of the background papers and make sure you like how it looks. Then, adhere the background elements together and add the cat drawing on top. If you use a glue stick, wait until the glue has dried completely before moving on to the next step.

16. Using pencil and a ruler, draw in the corner of the wall and the planks in the wood. Richard was helping.

17. Add in the cast shadows with a black pen. Start with making long, vertical lines and then cross-hatch over the top. Add shadow around and underneath the cat to ground the figure and make the background recede back into space.

18. Add in the wood grain texture. Look carefully at the source photo and notice the grain and variations in value. Add some long vertical lines into the darker planks. Then, using a shorter, scribbly mark, make some patches of grain. Don't feel like you have to follow perfectly what you see in the photo, just be sure that the marks follow the angle of the planks. Repeat in the lighter planks, but keep your marks lighter in value.

19. Create contrast between the planks by adding cross-hatching to the dark ones. Vary the length and concentration of hatches to make it look more natural. If needed, add some more perpendicular shading along the edges to make them contrast with the light planks.

20. With the drawing mostly finished, step back and look at the drawing as a whole. Is there anywhere that needs to go darker or needs more refining? The wall area on the left side seemed too stark, so I added some shading there. I also shaded around the sketchbook and darkened the cat's cast shadows.

21. Add in the whiskers with a white gel pen. Notice how they grow out of the dark spots around the nose. Flick your wrist at the end to make them come to a finer point. You only need to draw a few to get the point across. The gel pen can also be used to show the fur that sticks up off the face, ears, and body. Most importantly, Sir Richard gave his approval.

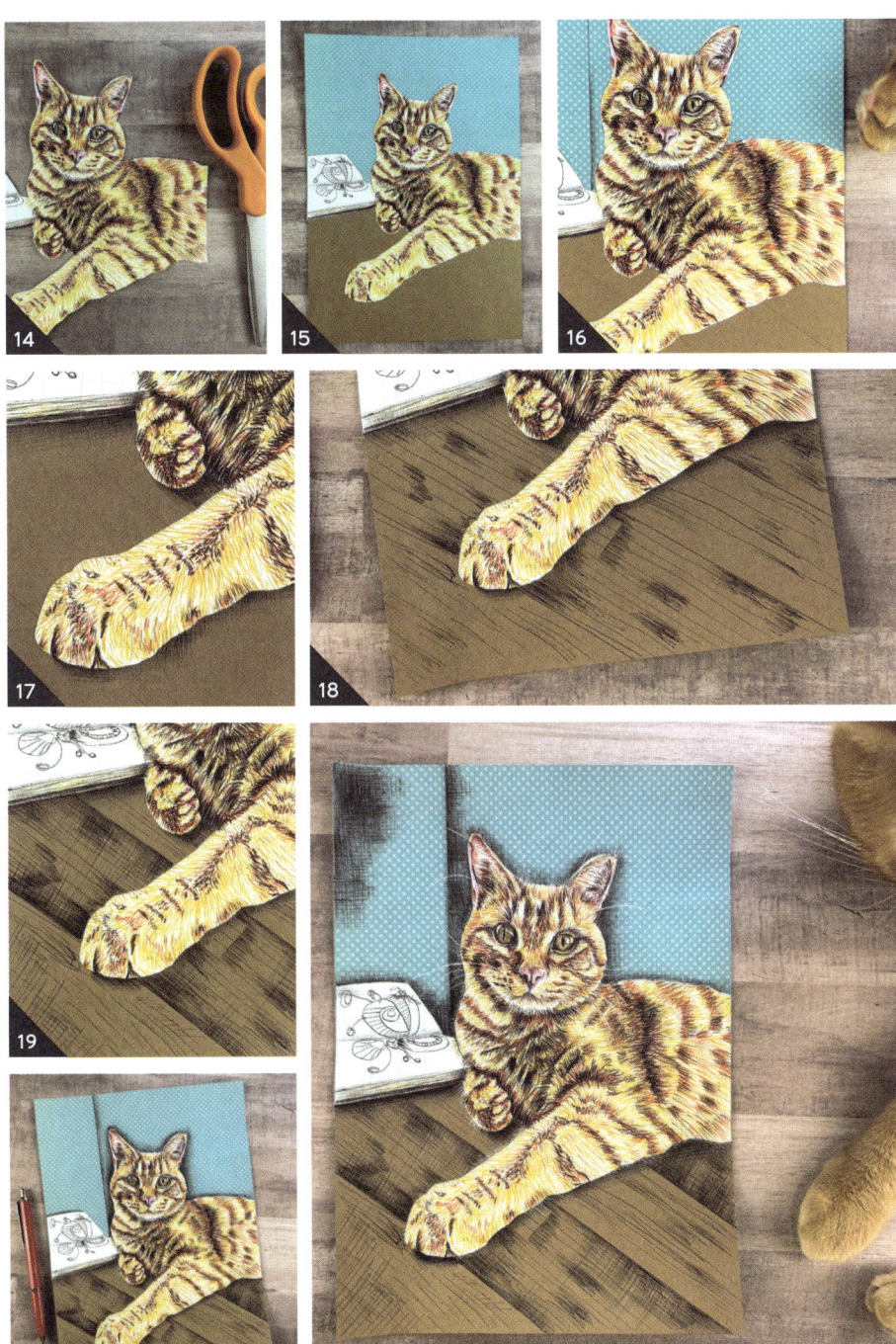

# FLORAL

Great ideas sometimes come about by accident, and that was certainly the case for this drawing. I originally intended to build a collage of flowers for this exercise, but when I got caught up in the detail of one single daisy, I changed course. The same thing happened with the marker background. When I realized the only blue marker I had on hand was a washable one, the marker background became a watercolor instead. As this drawing is quite detailed, I suggest working large so that it's easier to capture it.

## YOU WILL NEED

- 9 x 9in (23 x 23cm) or larger mixed media paper or hot press watercolor paper
- Image of a daisy at least as large as above
- Green fine-point pen
- Pencil
- Eraser
- Washable or watercolor markers in yellow, blue, and purple
- Soft watercolor brush
- Jar of water

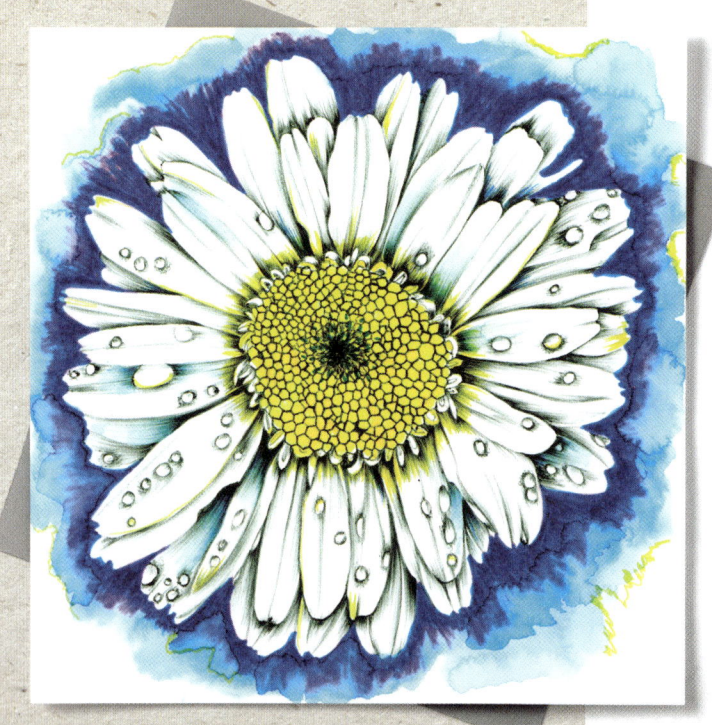

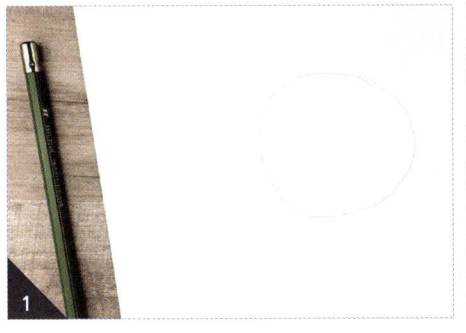

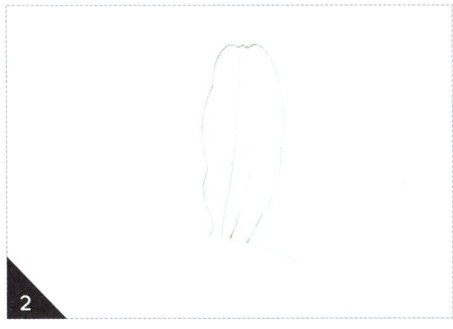

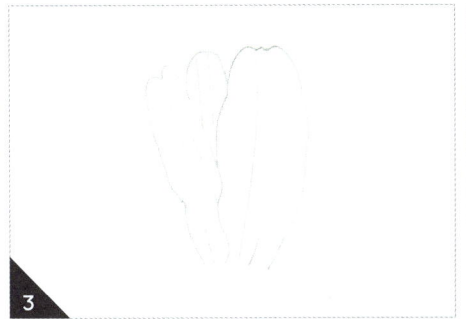

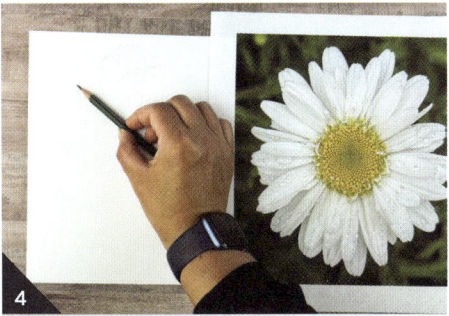

1. Using a pencil and a light touch, draw a circle in the center of the paper to approximate the central yellow structure. If you want to challenge yourself and speed up the process, do the rest of your drawing in pen, or continue in pencil.

2. Choose one single petal and draw its outline. Notice the subtle curves of the outer edge. Draw in the fine lines that run through the petal.

3. Draw the adjacent petals, noticing how they touch and overlap the petal you just drew. Don't worry about perfection, just draw shapes that approximate what you see in the photo. Use the lines in the petals to break down the shapes even further.

4. To get the proportions right, use your pencil as a measuring tool. Hold it up to the photo and use your fingers to mark the length of a petal. Then, move your hand to the drawing and align your fingers with the center circle and make a light mark with the pencil where it lies.

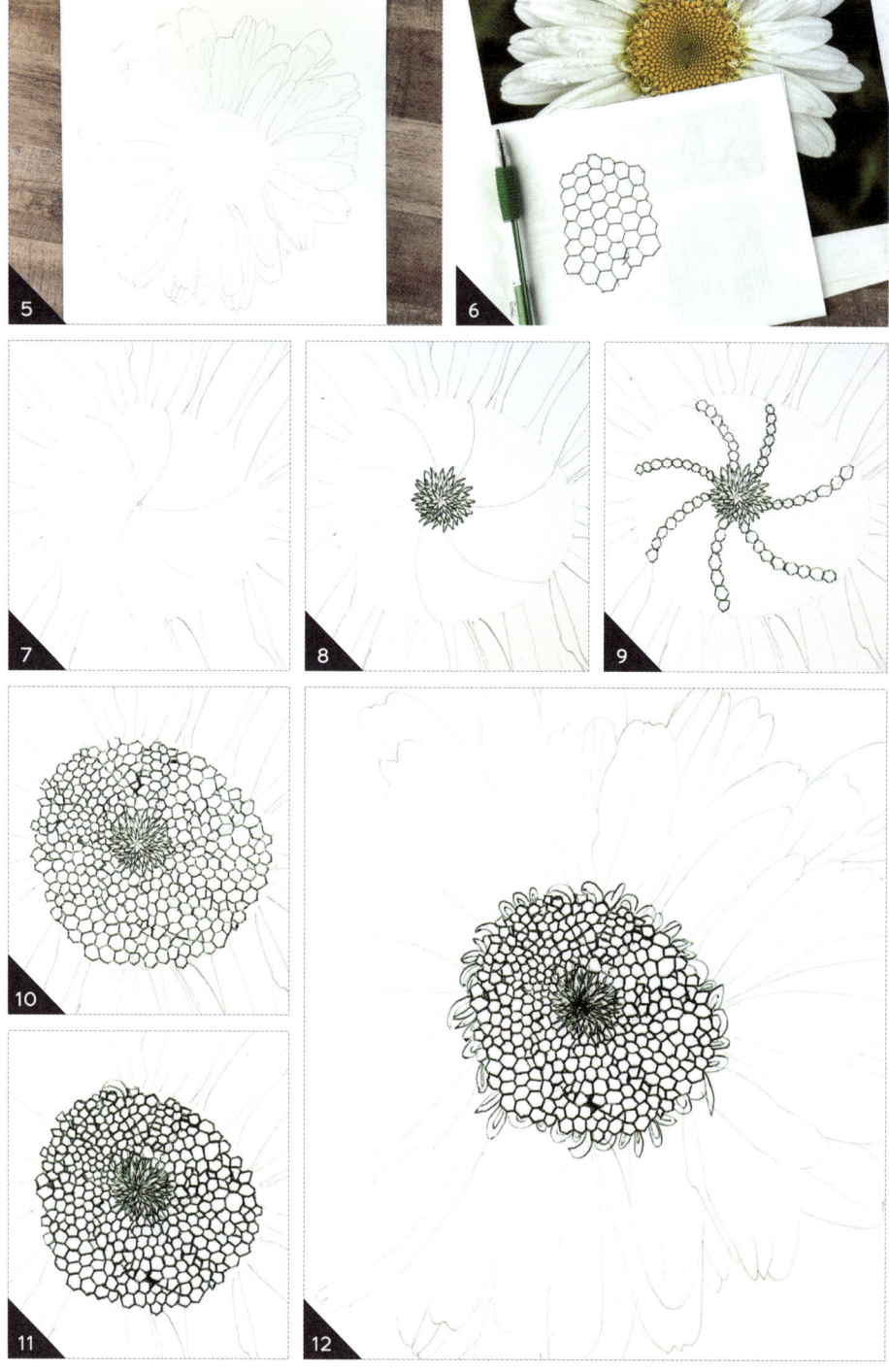

5. Keep working your way around the circle, one petal after another. If you can't fit all of the petals, oh well. No one will know!

6. Look closely at the pattern and structure of the yellow center. On a piece of scratch paper, practice drawing the hexagon shape and how they fit together in a honeycomb pattern. Keep going until drawing the pattern and shape feels comfortable.

7. In pencil, make a dot in the center of the circle. Lightly draw some curved lines that resemble the stripes on a peppermint.

8. Using a green pen, draw tiny "v" shapes around the center point. Keep going around in circles until you've drawn three or four rows.

9. Transition into hexagons that follow the curve of the pencil lines. Make each successive hexagon a bit larger than the one before it.

10. Fill in the space between the rows with more hexagons. As you are drawing freehand, the pattern won't look perfectly symmetrical, but that will only make it look more natural. As the outer edge of the center is somewhat jagged, vary the end point of the hexagons. If you're starting to go cross-eyed, be sure to take a break!

11. Trace over the "v" shapes and hexagons to thicken and darken them. This is quite a time-consuming process, so feel free to skip it. It won't affect your finished drawing very much, I promise!

12. Using a seed-like shape, draw the bracts around the edge of the center. Draw only the most prominent bracts instead of trying to draw every single one. Make sure that some point in towards the center and others point out towards the petals.

## TOP TIP

Close observation is truly the key to drawing realistically. As you draw, think less about what you're drawing and focus on drawing shapes that you see. Work from overlapping shape to overlapping shape for the best results.

**13.** Add shading to the petals. Start with the darkest shadows, shading where a petal runs underneath another. The goal is to obscure the outlines by creating contrast between overlapping shapes. Keep the shading on the light side for now. Use the photo to help you see where to shade.

**14.** Keep the rounded, most outer edges of the petals white for now. Draw in the most prominent water droplets with light pencil lines, but don't shade them.

**15.** Use a yellow marker to color in the center. Also add a bit of yellow around and inside of some of the bracts.

**16.** Turn your focus to the water droplets. Look closely at the darks and lights in and around them and shade those areas just as you did the petals. Use a smooth shading technique or scribble if that feels easier.

**17.** To make the white outer edges of the petals stand out, add some color to the background with a dark washable marker. Outline the white edges of the petals and then use a loose scribble to quickly fill in the space. To add some variety and darken the background a bit, layer in another color.

**18.** With a soft watercolor brush, paint over the background with clean water. The more water you add, the more it will flow and bloom. Let the paper dry thoroughly before moving on.

**19.** To tie the background and flower together, add small amounts of blue marker to the darks in the flower including the darkest part of the center. Lastly, add some yellow to the light areas of the petals and to the background. You can also add water to some areas to allow the color to flow.

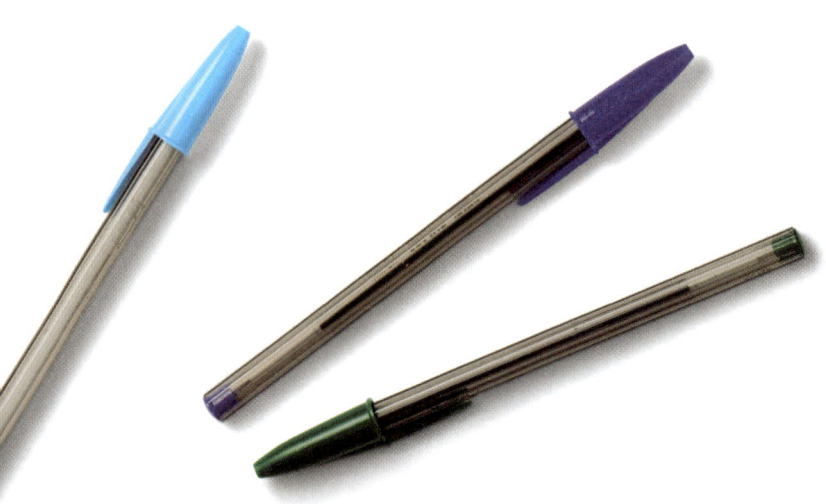

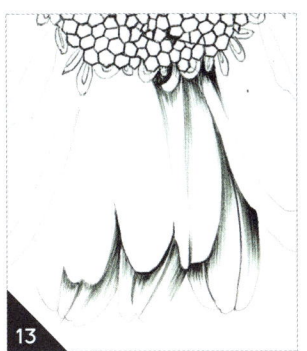

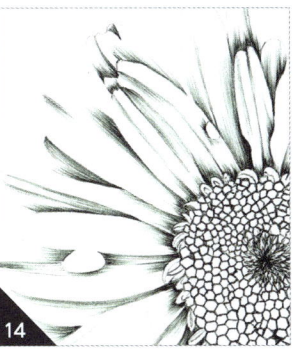

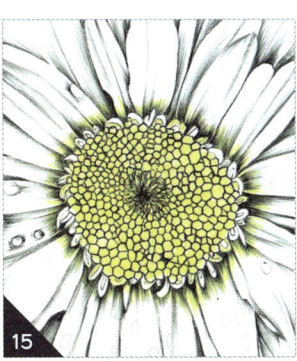

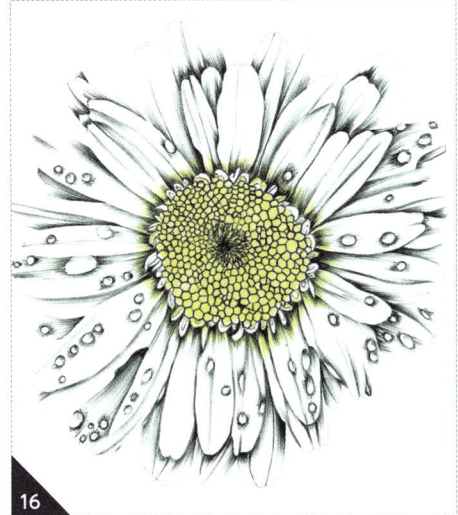

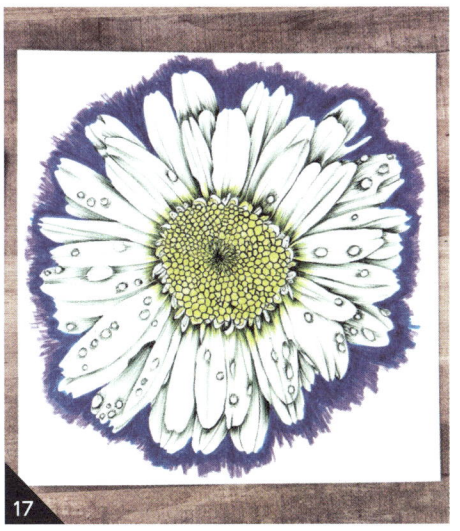

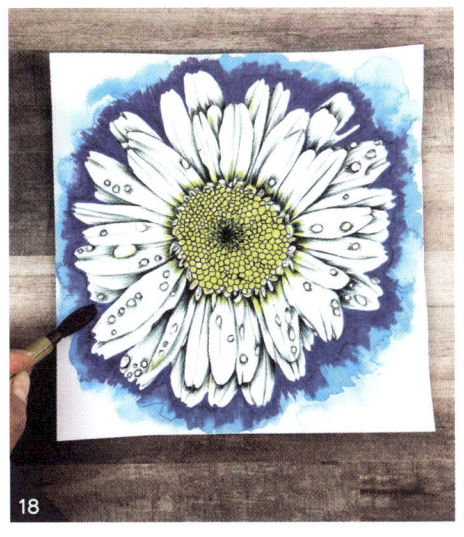

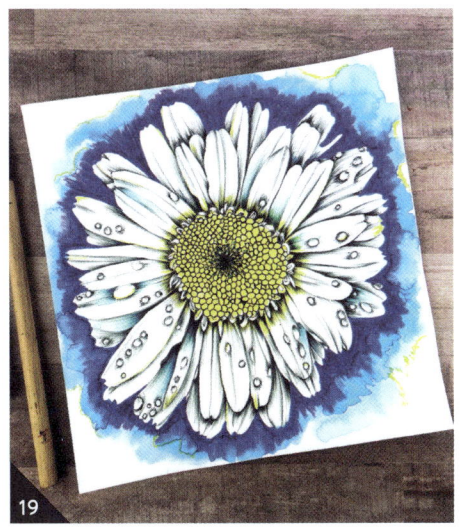

# LANDSCAPE

It's not necessary to start with a majestic vista to create an interesting, lush landscape drawing. This photo was taken in the fall at a local forest preservation. Though the color isn't terribly exciting, the composition is strong and the play of the larger tree and water shapes contrast nicely with the ground cover and the small foliage in the background. In this exercise, you'll use mark making in an impressionist manner to craft a rich, loose landscape.

## YOU WILL NEED

- 6 x 8in (15 x 20cm) smooth Bristol board or marker paper
- Landscape photo
- Wide-point pens in a range of colors (black, brown, blue, green, orange, and yellow)
- Pencil
- Eraser

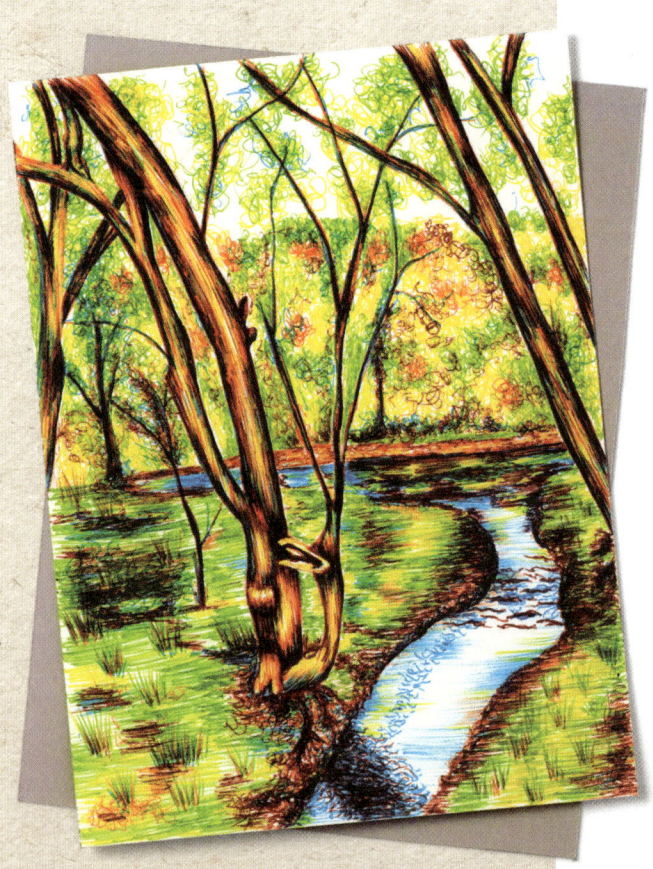

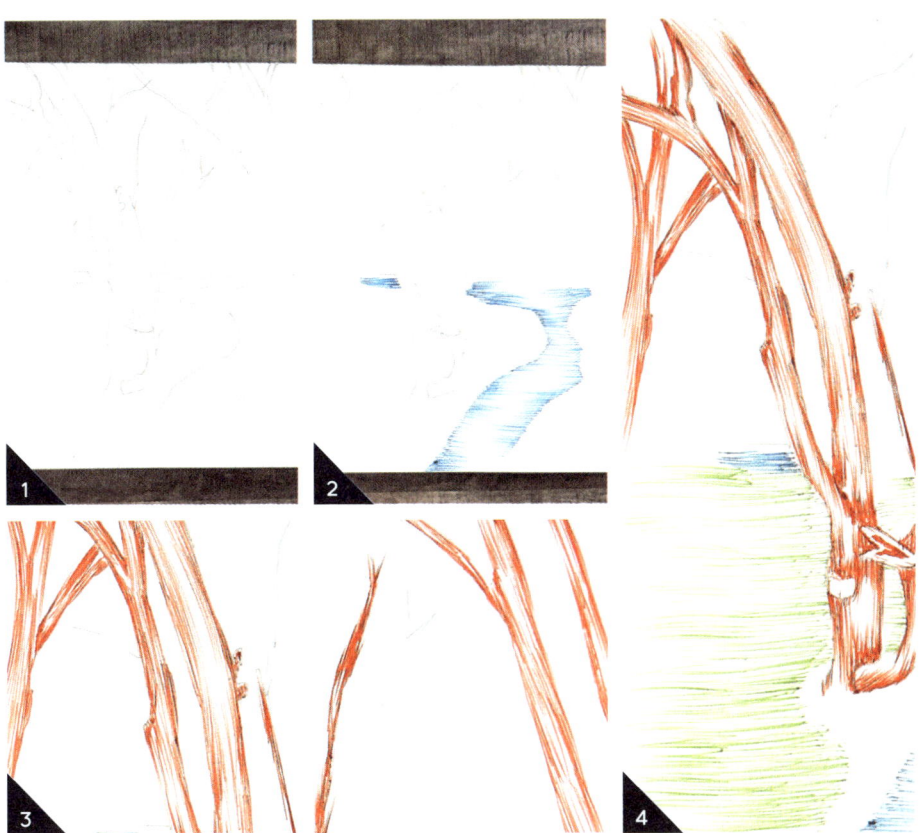

1. Using a pencil, sketch in the major shapes, including the edges of the river and the largest branches of the tree. Draw the negative spaces between the branches instead of the tree itself. Keep it simple and the lines light.

2. Starting with a light blue pen and a horizontal stroke, lightly shade in the water. To give the composition a bit more balance, I added a touch of blue to the left of the main tree, even though it's not there in the photo.

3. With a mostly vertical mark that runs parallel to the trunk, shade the tree bark in brown. Use a rusty color instead of a true brown, if you can, to inject more color into the drawing. Shade darker towards the edges and lighter towards the middle. Ignore the finer branches at this point.

4. With a horizontal mark, add in the ground cover with a green pen. Keep it light and open so other colors and marks can be added later.

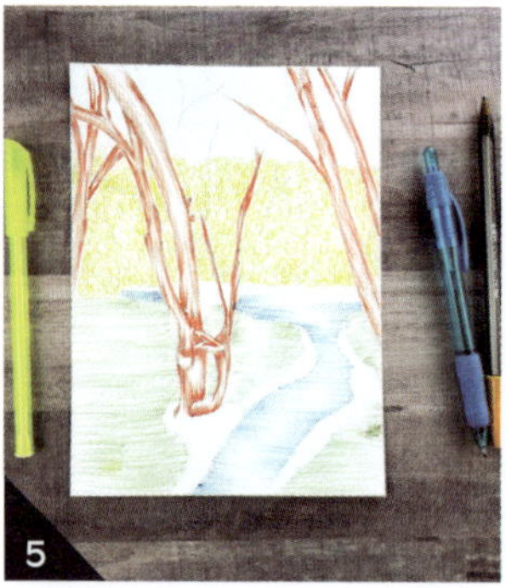

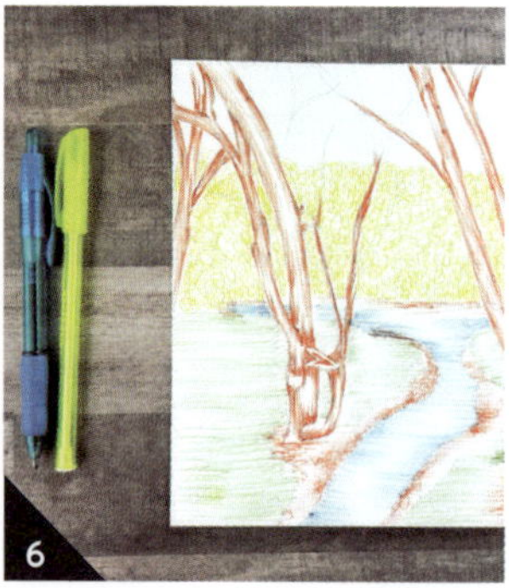

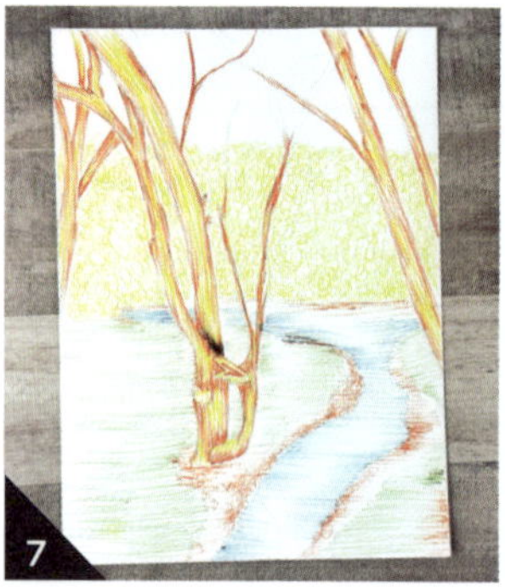

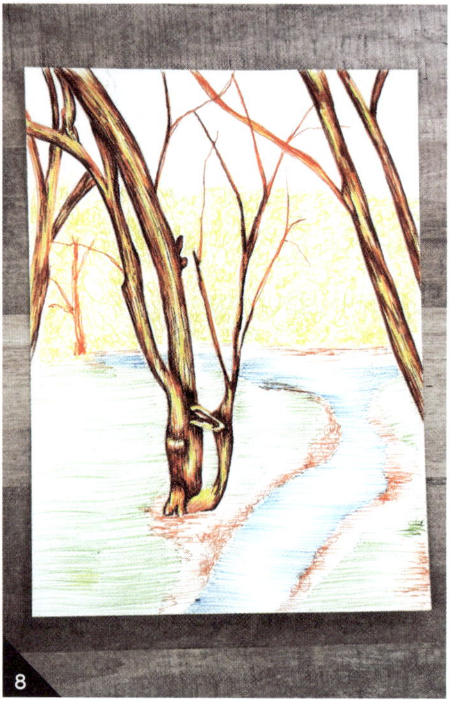

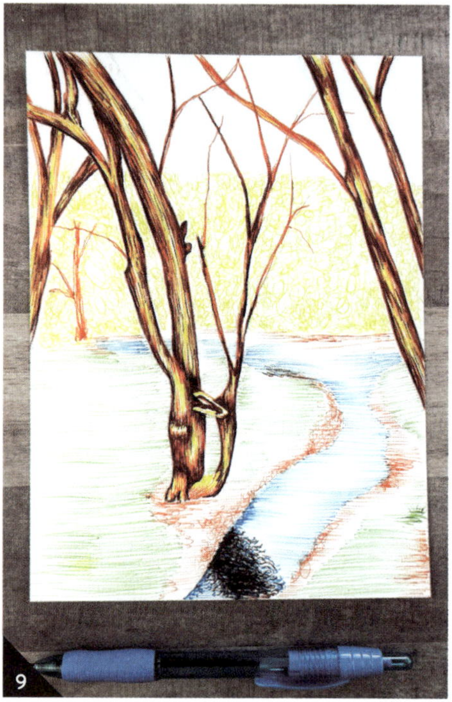

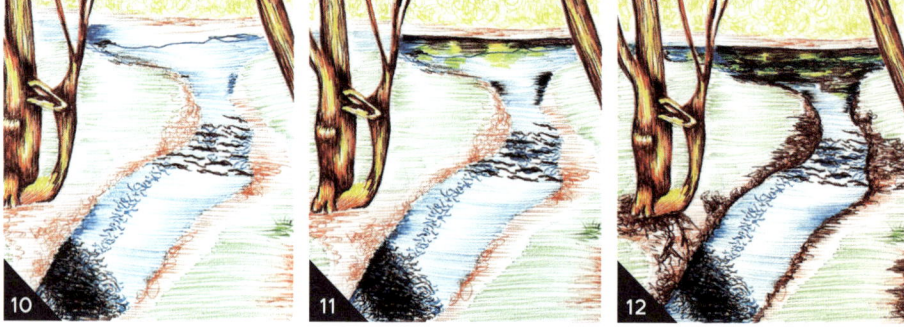

5. Use an orange or yellow to scribble in the brush in the background.

6. Fill in the muddy shoreline with the same color that you used on the tree. Use a mix of scribbles and horizontal lines.

7. Add yellow to the middle of the branches to make them appear round. If you don't have a yellow, orange will suffice as a lighter tone.

8. Using a darker brown, layer in some darks along the edges of the trees. Use a mark that mimics the texture of the bark. Add in more of the rust and yellow as needed.

9. Turn your attention to the water, adding blue and then brown into the shadow cast by the tree. Use a squiggle shape around the edges of the shadow to mimic the ripples in the water.

10. Repeat the squiggle shape in blue where you see it in the water. With brown and a longer squiggle, draw in the darker ripples.

11. Continue to fill in the dark areas of water with brown. As you work along the shoreline, layer in some yellow and light green that's reflected in the water.

12. To make the light areas of the water stand out and to define the shoreline, enhance the darks with some brown scribbles.

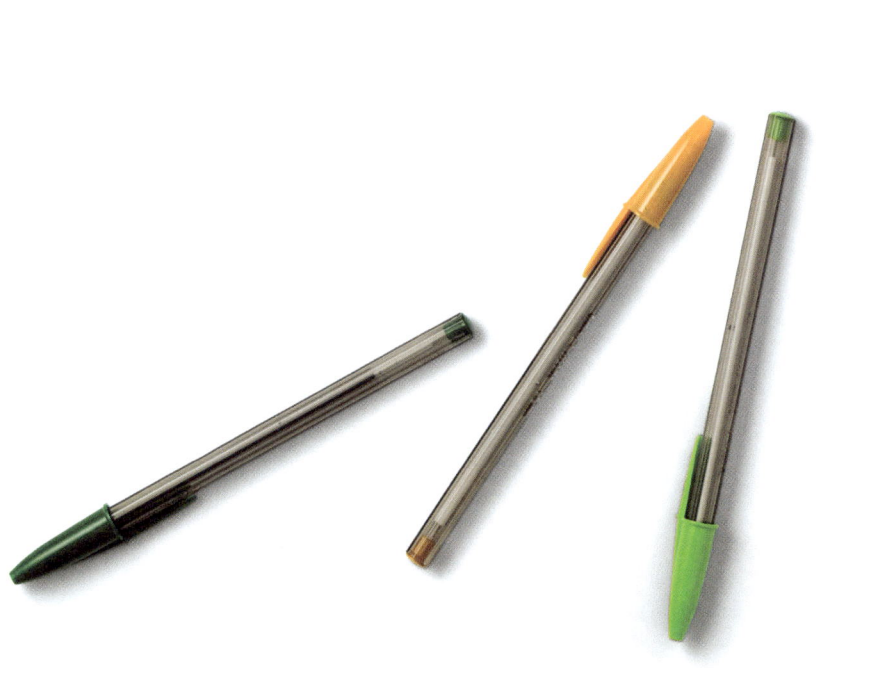

13. Fill in the grassy areas with a mix of yellow, light green, and touches of brown and rust. In the background, use a horizontal stroke to push it back in space. Towards the foreground, incorporate vertical tufts of grass.

14. Fill in the leaves in the background with scribbles. Layer in oranges, greens, and brown on top of the existing yellow, varying the amounts and concentrations of each.

15. Add more color to the shoreline using rust, brown, and yellow.

16. Now that almost every part of the drawing has been filled in, start to enhance the darks. Start by adding blue to tree trunks in dashes to give the appearance of bark. Darken in the smallest branches as well.

17. Using a scribble, add yellow, blue, and green to the sky, along the branches, to create leaves. Be sure to leave some white space so there is still some sky visible. Darken in the brush so that it contrasts with the sky. Adding in some brown and blue should do the trick.

18. To pull all the elements of the drawing together, add bits of blue and orange to the grass, and yellow and orange to the water. Just a little bit will make a difference.

## TOP TIP

Instead of using black to create dark values, try using complementary colors to darken (like adding blue to orange.) This will create a more rich, earthy dark.

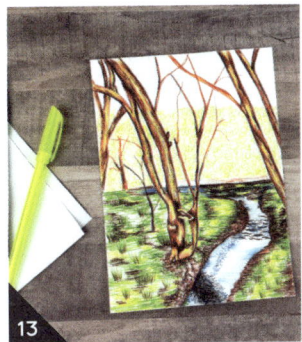

13

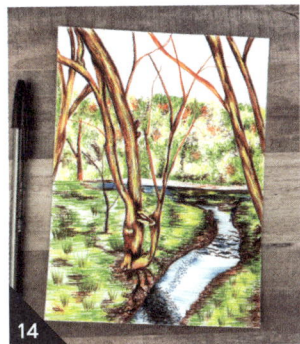

14

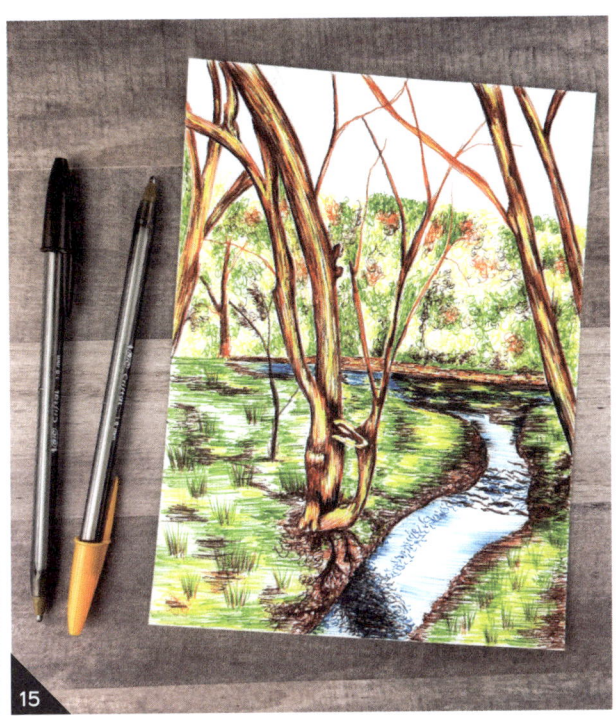

15

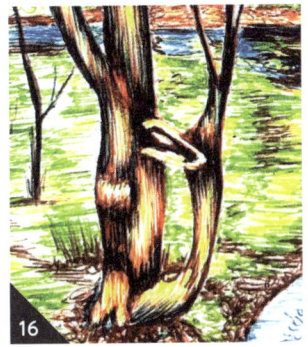

16

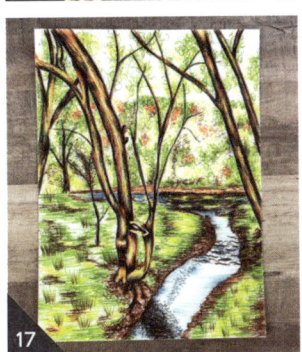

17

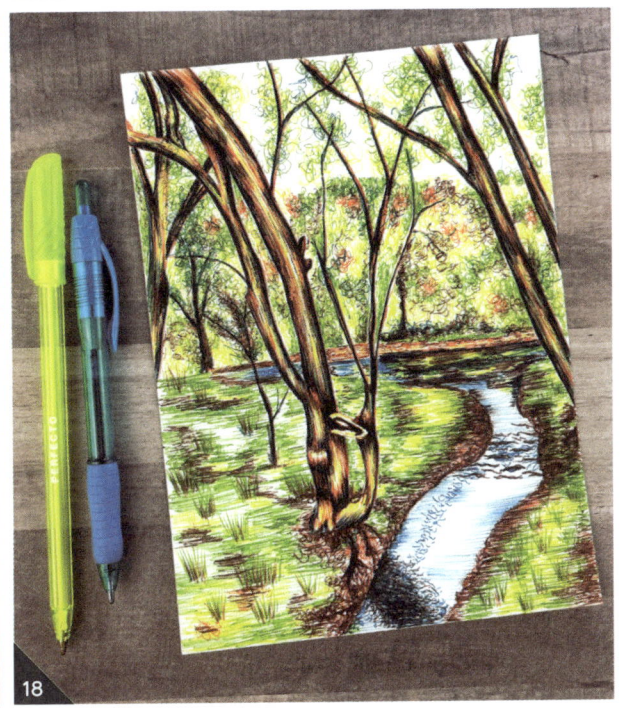

18

# PORTRAIT

I took this photo while on a trip to Kenya, where I taught art to children in a school in Nairobi. I'd often catch these two watching through the window – they were so interested in what we were doing. The sweet expression on the girl's face and how the light falls makes her ideal for a pen drawing. As in other projects, we'll be using collage to add the color.

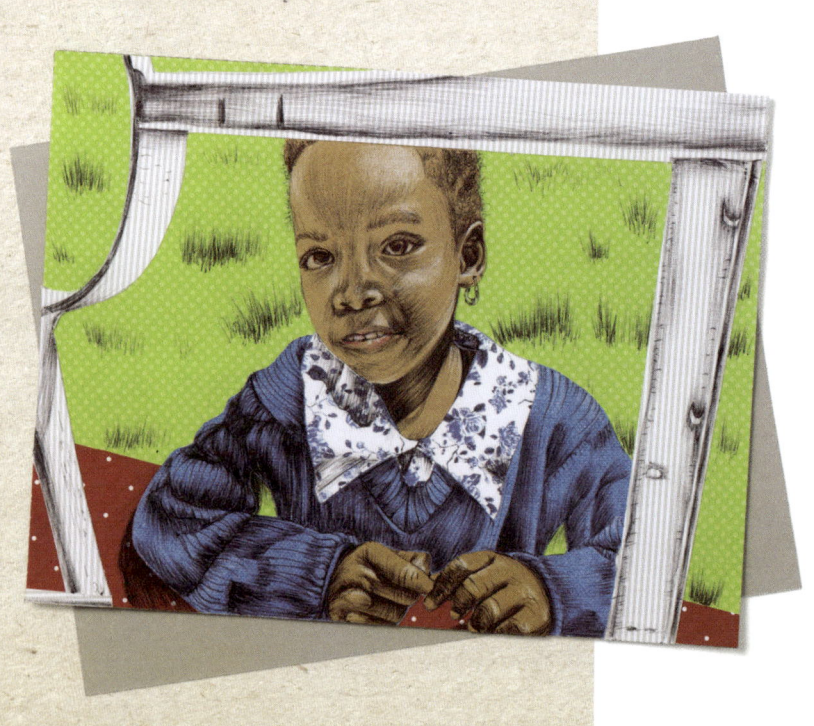

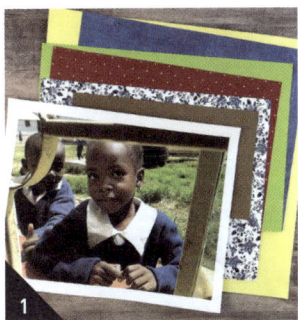 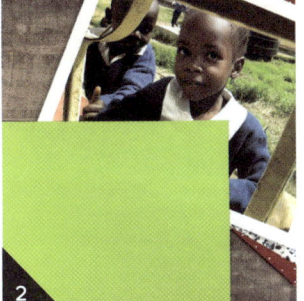 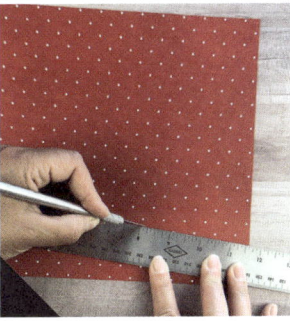

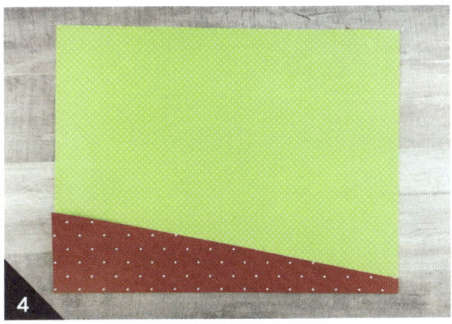 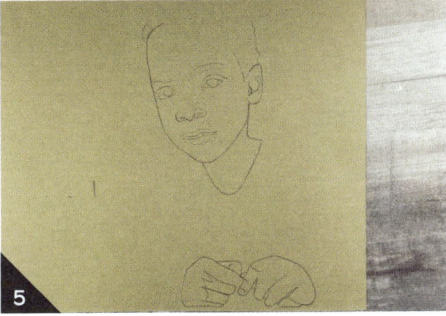

1. Select some papers to represent the different colors from your source photo in the drawing.

2. Print out the source photo at the size of your final drawing and cut your background paper to that size. I used a light green to represent the grass.

3. Cut the next paper, in this case for the window ledge. I measured the height on the left edge of the photo and used that as a starting point for my cut. Using a craft knife and a ruler, cut the paper at a diagonal.

4. Use glue or double-sided mounting film to adhere the "window ledge" to the bottom edge of the background paper.

5. Choose a base color for the face and hands. Lay the source photo on top of the paper, sandwiching some carbon paper in between. Secure the photo to the paper with some low-tack masking tape. Trace over the major features of the face and hands with a sharp pencil.

## TOP TIP

Use glue for the smaller collage elements and mounting film for the larger elements that could warp if you use glue on them.

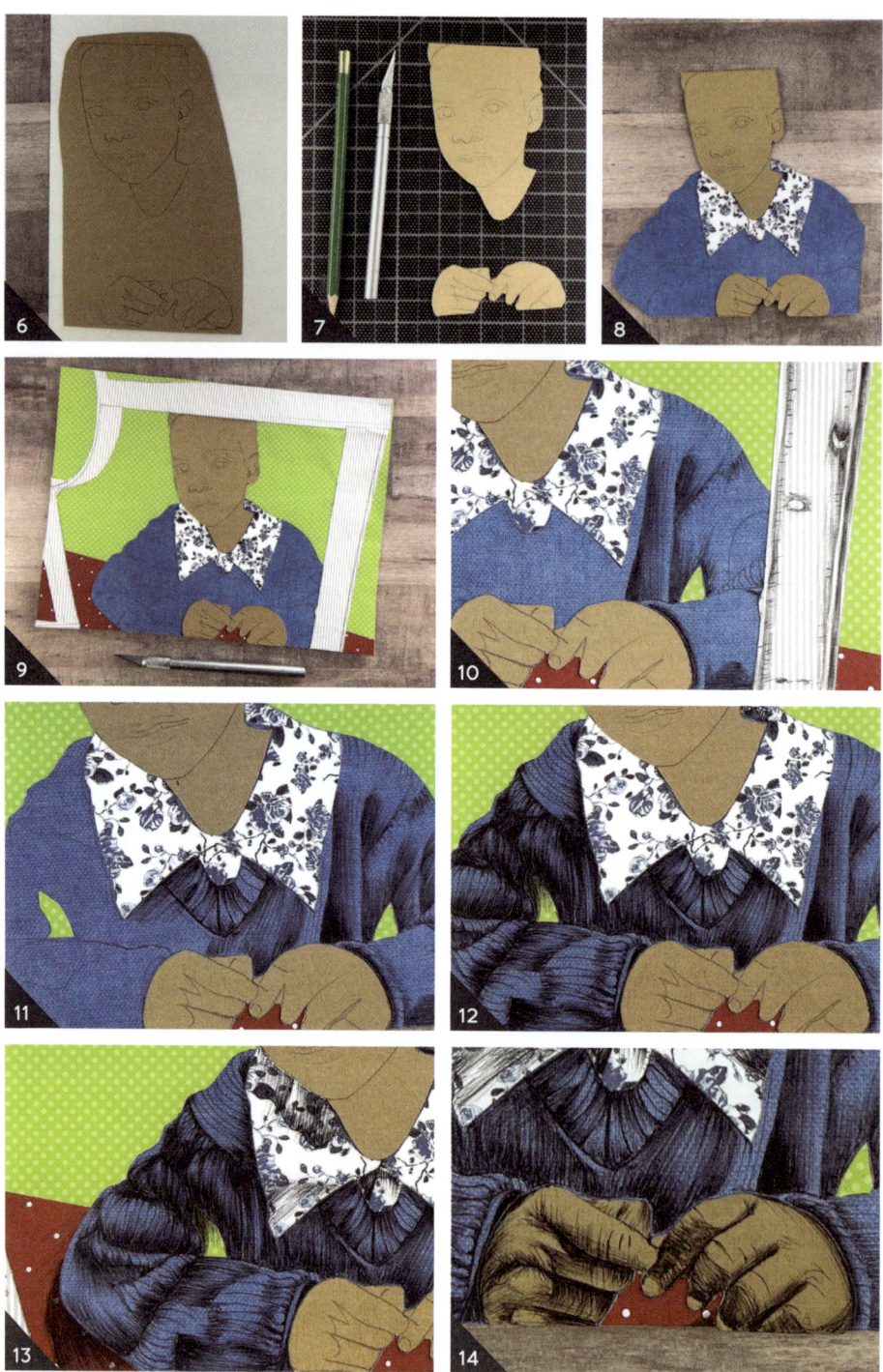

6. If you're using mounting film to adhere the layers, roughly cut out the face and hands, leaving a border around them. Then cut the mounting film to approximately the same size and adhere to the back side of the drawing. If you're using a glue stick, you can skip this step.

7. With a sharp craft knife, carefully cut out the face and hands. Cut just inside the outlines so you don't have to worry about obscuring them later.

8. Draw the shape of the collar onto the paper you've chosen and cut it out. Repeat the process with the sweater, but don't cut away the space where the collar and neck overlap. Glue the collar, face, and hands onto the sweater.

9. Finish the collage by gluing the whole figure to the background, then cut and adhere the window frame to the figure and background.

10. With a black wide-point pen, begin to shade the collage. Add in the shadows of the window frame, including some of the little imperfections, to give it some interest and character. Shade in the dark areas of the sweater to illustrate the folds. Shade in the direction of the knitting for a more realistic look.

11. As I was shading, I realized that I had forgotten to cut away the small triangles of space formed by the arms. I cut bits of the green background paper and glued them in place. It's another good way to deal with any mistakes.

12. Add in some lines to suggest the texture of the knit in the lighter areas, noticing how the lines curve around the folds and edges.

13. Lightly shade in the collar, adding value where the face casts a shadow. Also create the cast shadow under the elbow.

14. Now that you're warmed up, move on to the hands. It's a good time to switch to a fine-point pen for this detailed work. Use a rounded mark that wraps around the fingers to give them dimension.

---

**TOP TIP**

Lighten up the contrast of the photo to get a better view of the details.

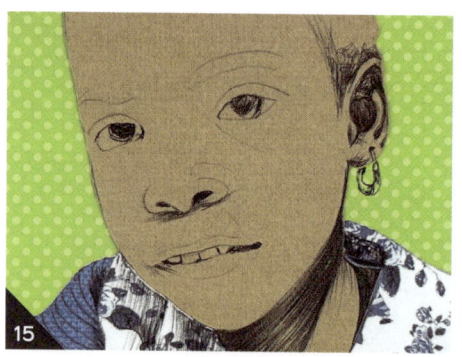

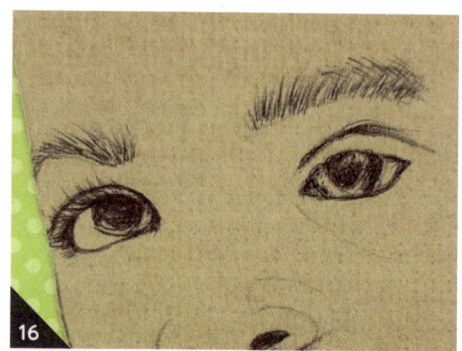

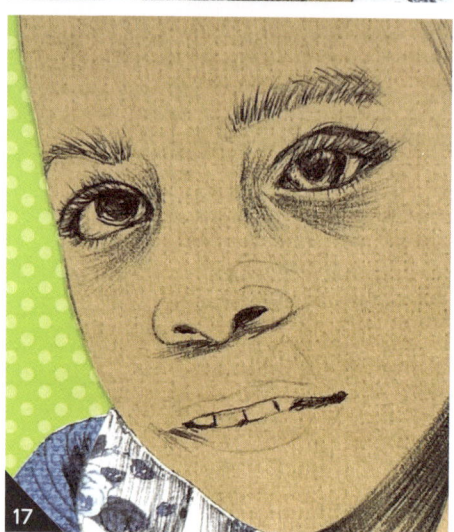

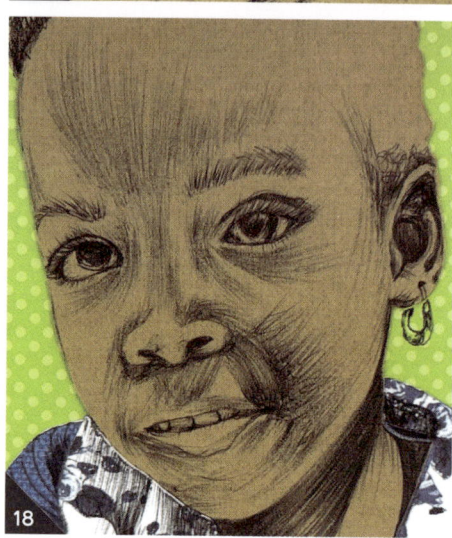

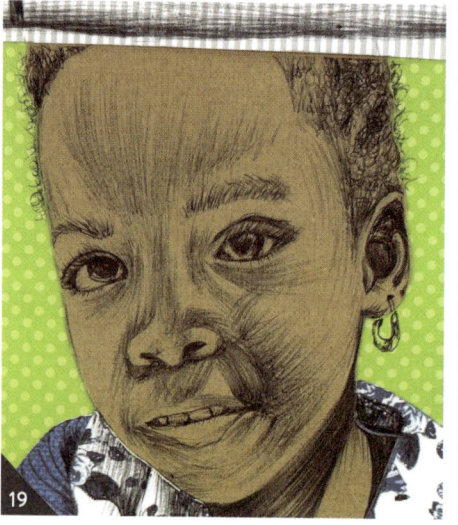

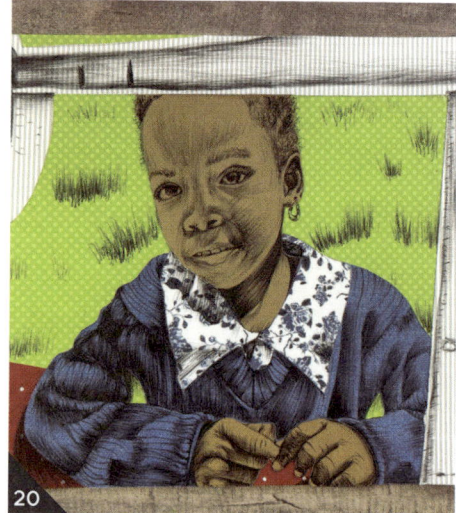

15. Moving to the face, consider working upside down. You'll see it less as a face and more as a collection of darks and lights. Start by shading in the darkest areas first. Fill in the inside of the ear, pupils and irises of the eyes, the nostrils, and corners of the mouth. From there, work from feature to feature around the face.

16. To form the eyebrows, use fine, light lines that point up and out from the nose. To create the arch, add lines on the outside edges of the brow that point down and out from the forehead. Notice the darks in the corners and around the edges of the whites of the eyes, shading those in first. Use a soft touch to add in the dark crease above the eye.

17. Next add the eyelashes with fine lines that sweep up and curve out towards the outer edges of the eye. Add a few bottom lashes at the outer edges. To describe the thickness of the eyelid, leave a light edge and then shade underneath the eye and on the bridge of the nose.

18. As there are very few sharp edges in the nose and ears, keep the shading soft. Refer to your photo to see where to shade. Connect the nose to the mouth area by adding in the shadows that give roundness to the cheeks. So that the teeth look like they are inside the mouth, add some shading to them. Define the lips with shadow, avoiding sharp edges. With a very light touch, add some shading to the cheeks and forehead. Don't worry if it looks heavy handed at this point.

19. Use a mix of a scribble and a short straight line to describe the texture of the hair. Vary the concentration of the marks to create darker and lighter areas. To soften the edge of the hairline, add a small amount of scribble onto the green background.

20. Add some tufts of grass to the green background, to give it some interest and depth.

21. To bring the face to life, it needs some highlights, added with a white colored pencil. Squint at the face, to see the lightest areas of the photo and add white there. Use white sparingly in the teeth and eyes. Instead, concentrate on the forehead, cheek, upper lip, ear, and earring. Adding a touch of pink colored pencil (or pen) to the lips brings more life to the face as well. Finally, add some touches of white to the sweater and hands, and you're done!

21

# CHAIR

I have a thing for chairs and have been
illustrating them for years. They have
personality and style and often serve
as stand-ins for people in my work,
conveying a range of human emotions.
On top of that, chairs are just fun to draw.
In this project, you'll again use collage
paper to add the color and black pen for
the detail. I'll also share an alternative
transfer method using tracing paper.

## YOU WILL NEED

- Selection of colored and/
  or patterned paper
- Image of a chair
- Low-tack masking tape
- Tracing paper
- HB pencil
- Blue fine-point pen
- Black medium-point pen
- 8 x 8in (20.5 x 20.5cm)
  Bristol board
- Craft knife or scissors
- Double-sided mounting
  film or glue stick
- Scratch paper or paper
  towel
- Ruler

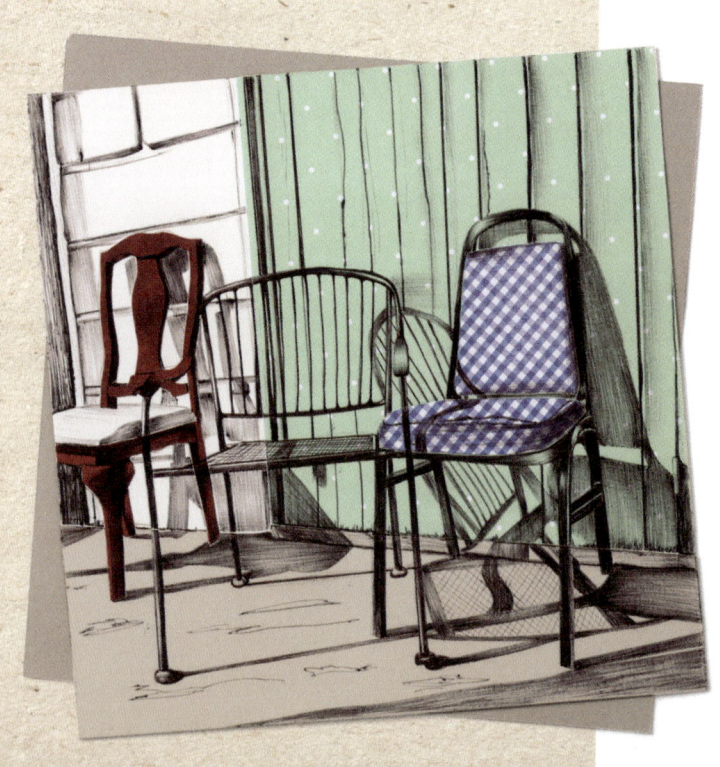

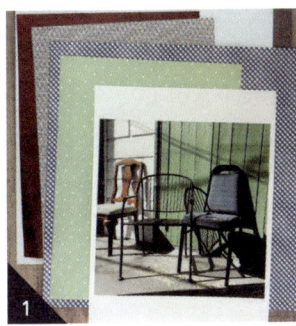
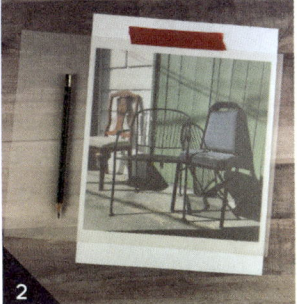
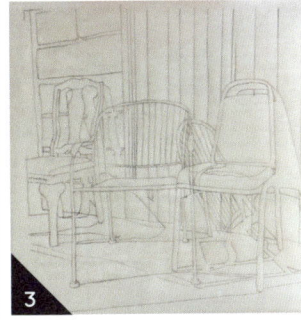
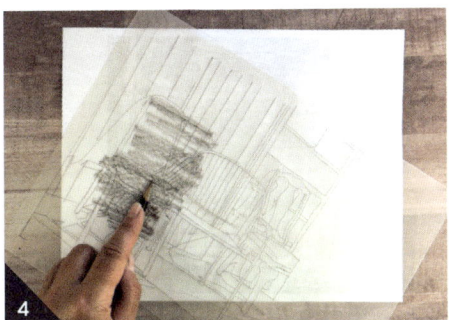
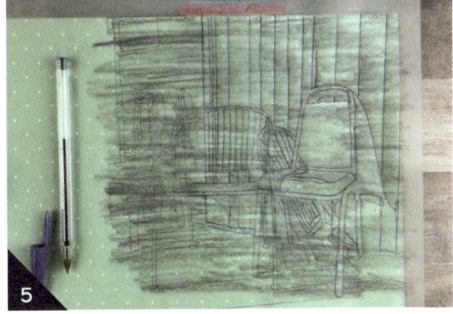

1. Select some smooth paper to represent the color from your source photo in the drawing. Print out the source photo at the size of your final drawing and cut the background paper to that size.

2. Lay a piece of tracing paper on top of the photo and secure it with low-tack masking tape.

3. With a sharp HB pencil, trace over all the major shapes in the photo. This can be tedious, so put on some good background music or a podcast and settle in. Work from one side of the photo to the other to avoid missing anything. Keep your pencil sharp so the lines stay crisp.

4. Turn the tracing paper over and apply a light layer of pencil all over the back of the drawing. Hold your pencil almost parallel to the paper and scribble. This will make up for all of the tracing you just did!

5. Tape the tracing paper (right side up) to the paper you want as the background. With a blue fine-point pen or pencil, retrace the lines. Use blue so you can keep track of what you've already traced. The pressure of your pen along with the graphite on the back of the tracing paper will transfer the lines onto the collage paper. Basically, you made your own carbon paper.

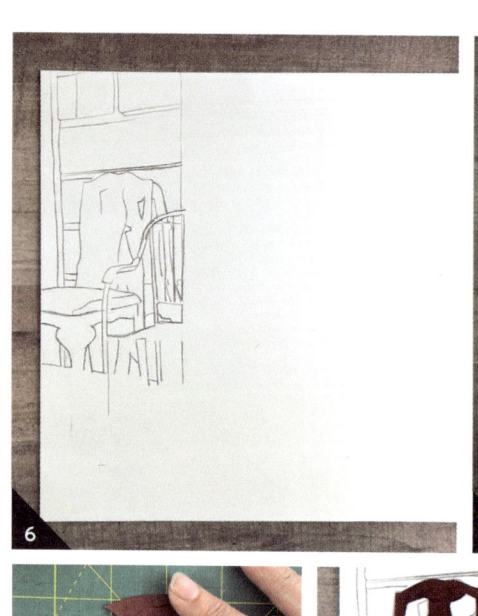

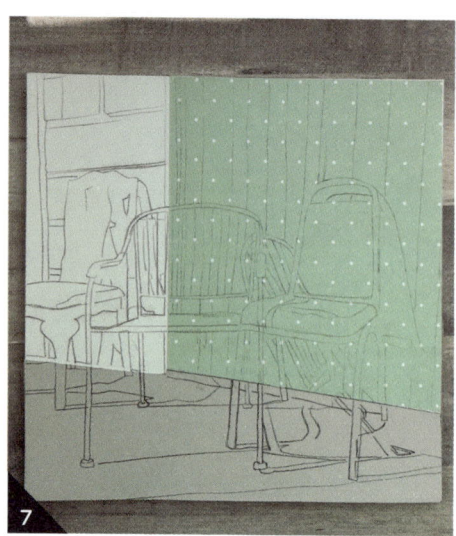

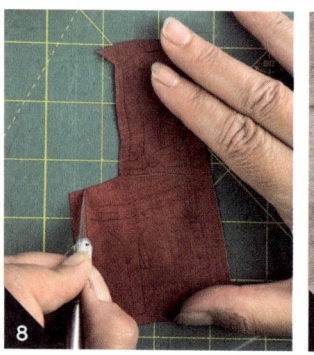

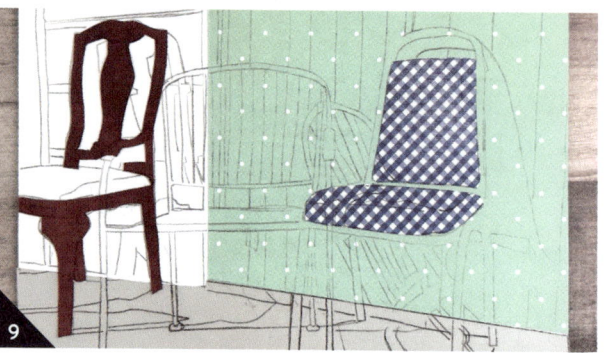

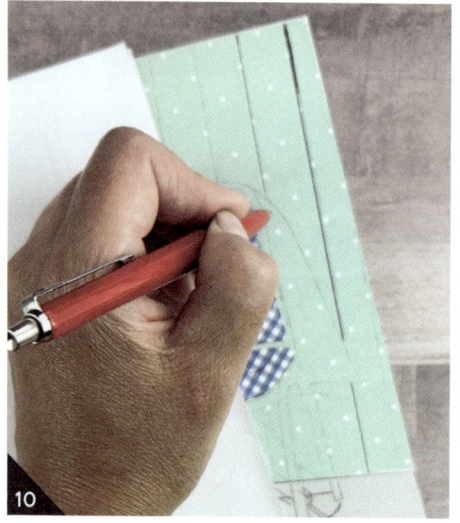

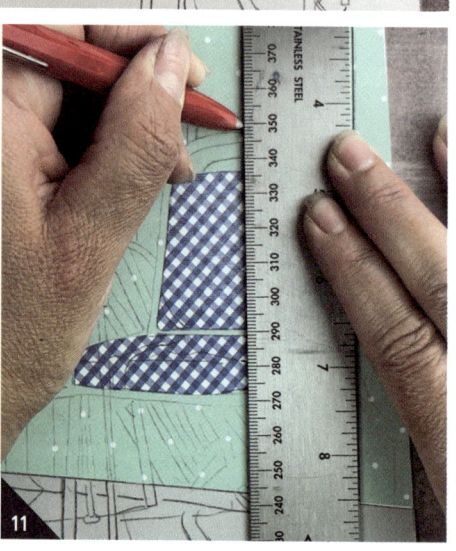

6. Repeat the process for the white area of the background, transferring it right onto the Bristol board. Just trace the outline of the wooden chair, so you know where to place the wood-colored paper later.

7. Transfer the legs of the chairs and shadows onto the paper you want for the ground and cut to size. Using double-sided mounting film or glue stick, adhere both the green and gray papers to the Bristol board.

8. Next, cut out the wood of the chair and the blue chair cushions by transferring the outlines onto your chosen papers. Don't cut out the pieces where the black chair overlaps.

9. Finish the collage by gluing down these last cut pieces.

10. Use your favorite black pen to do the shading. Work left to right if you are right-handed, and right to left if you are a lefty like me. Keep scratch paper or a paper towel under your hand. If you're having trouble making out any of the detail in a shadowed area, use a photo app on your phone or computer to lighten up the photo.

11. Use a ruler to make any straight edges truly straight. Alternatively, a little wiggle in your lines is okay too. It adds character and personality!

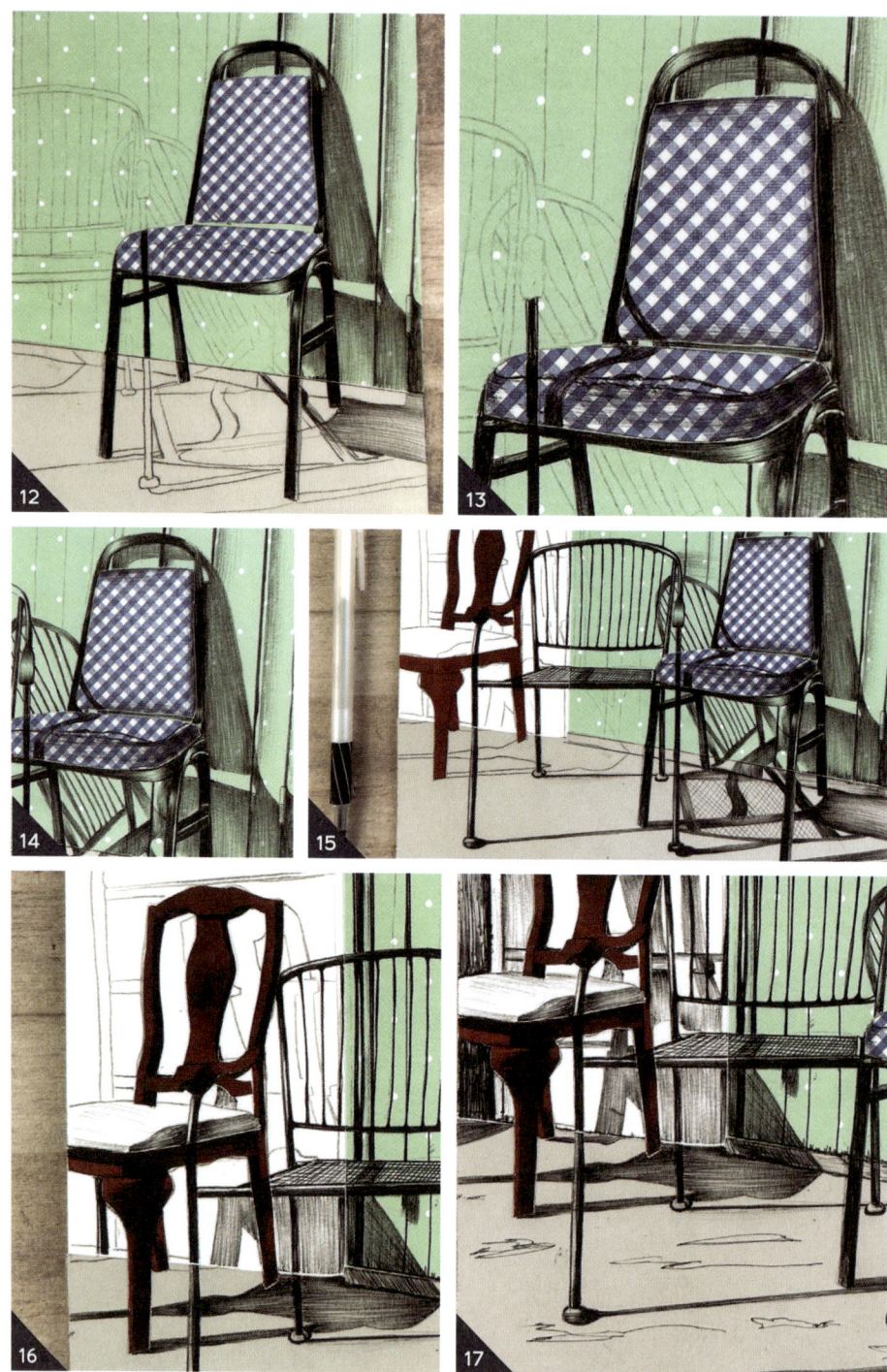

12. Fill in the black metal of the blue chair, not worrying too much about transitions. Do pay attention to the little highlights at the edges as these give the chair dimension. Just leave a little bit of paper showing in these spaces. Keep the cast shadows a bit lighter than the black metal.

13. To give the back cushion of the blue chair some dimension, create a transition from dark to light around the top, left, and bottom edges. Horizontally shade around the side and front edge of the seat cushion and add in the cast shadow from the metal chair.

14. Shade the cast shadows on the wall with mainly vertical strokes and shade horizontally on the ground. Try to use a cross-hatch in the cast shadows. Not all of the shadow has to be included to get the point across. For instance, you could easily omit the spindle shadows on the back of the green wall as they somewhat distract from the chairs themselves.

15. Approach the cast iron chair in the middle as you did the blue chair. Make it basically black, except for the visible highlights on the arms, seat, and right side of the back, leaving some paper showing. Round the ends of the spindle lines where they connect to the cross pieces of the chair back. Use a small cross-hatch to shade in and create the texture of the chair seat. Shade right over the wood/red paper where it overlaps with the chair.

16. Moving onto the wood chair, shade in the dark edges of the chair, with the red paper serving as the light. Add some shadow to the sides and edges of the cushion to give it roundness and contrast from the background.

17. Lastly, add in a bit of texture on the pavement. Use horizontal shapes that loosely mimic the peeling of the paint on the floor.

# CHAPTER 5
# ABSTRACT INSPIRATION

Though it may not be apparent in the final piece, most abstract art has a concrete subject behind it. It's hard to start from nothing! Abstract artists take their inspiration from nature, landscapes, architecture, or even portraiture. In this chapter, I'll share some simple techniques to inspire abstract drawings.

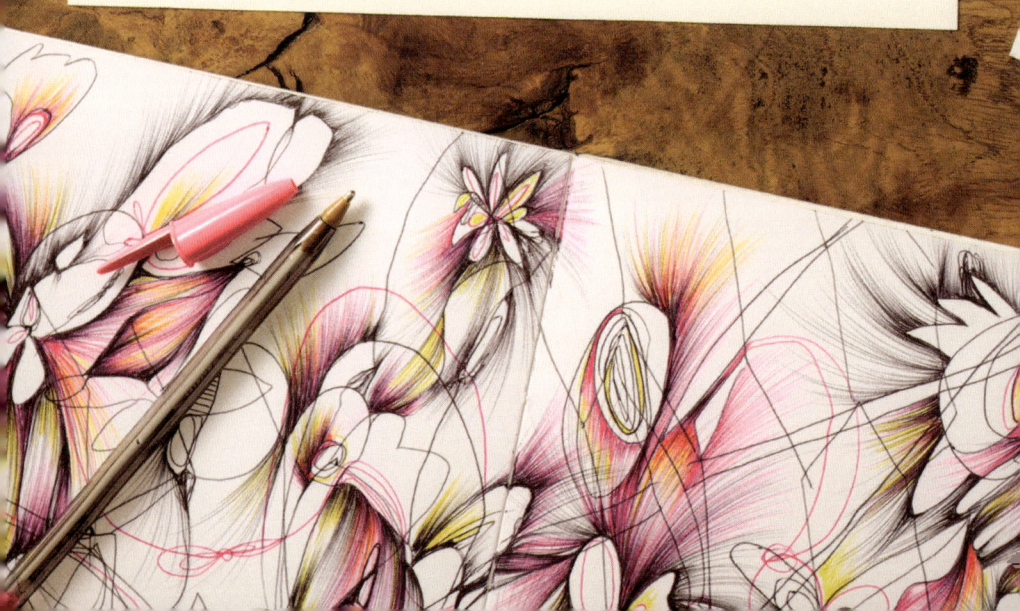

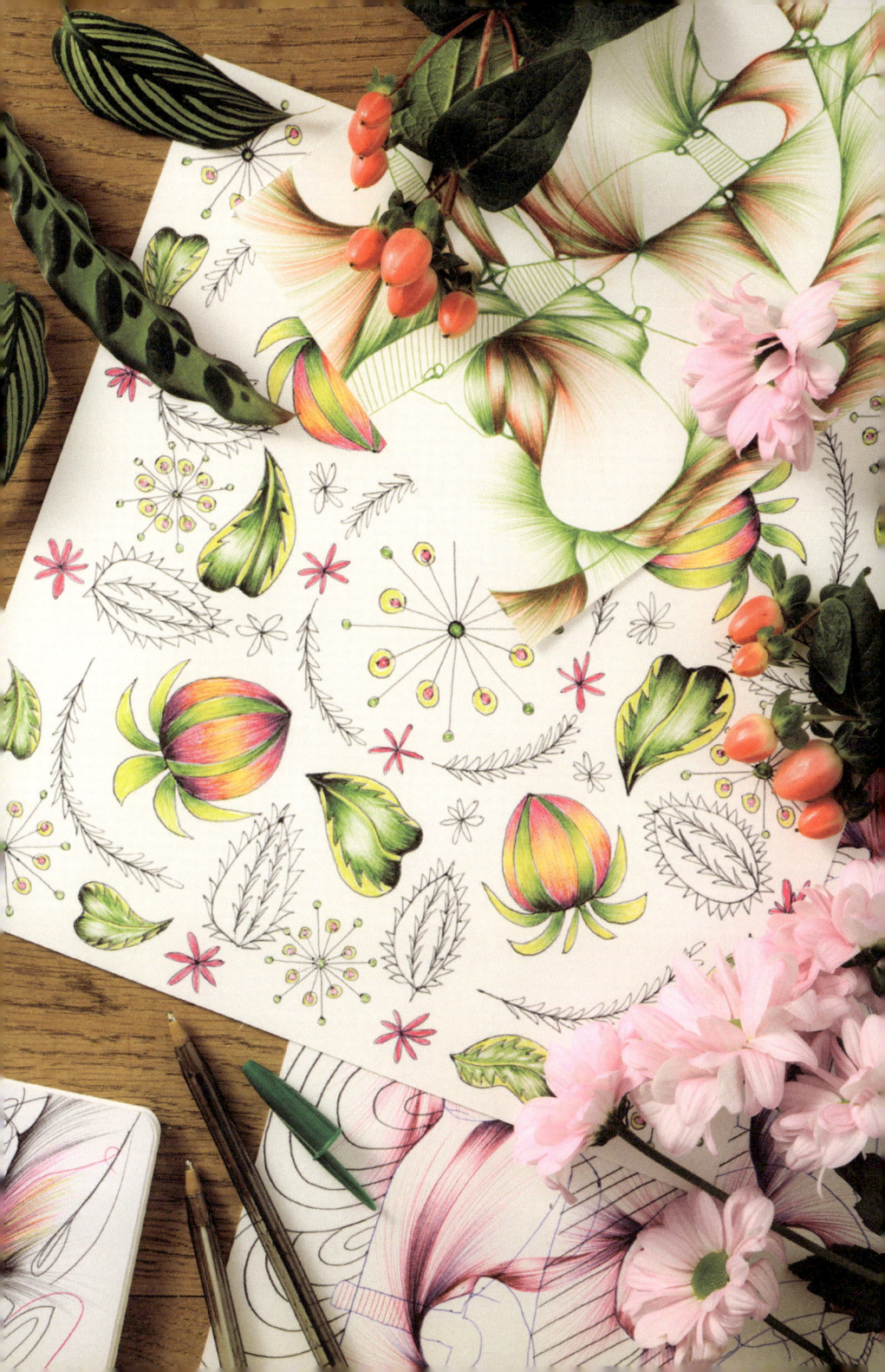

# ABSTRACT
## FROM SHADOWS

Shadows are a natural form of abstraction. Light diffused through trees, plants, and the built environment create gorgeous compositions on the pavement. In this project, I invite you to seek out the shadows in your surroundings, record them in your sketchbook, and use them as inspiration for an abstract drawing. Shadows are best captured in the early morning or later in the afternoon, when the light is at an angle.

## YOU WILL NEED

- Sketchbook or smooth paper
- Pens in a variety of widths and colors

### TOP TIP

It can be easy to work on an abstract incessantly as there's no real end point. When you feel you are done, walk away for a bit. When you come back with fresh eyes, you might see areas that need to be refined or it might just be done.

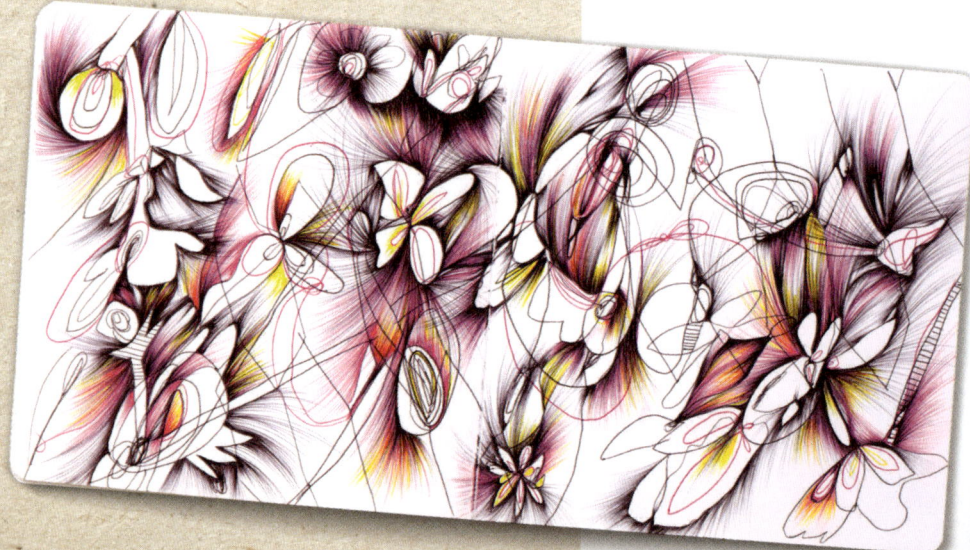

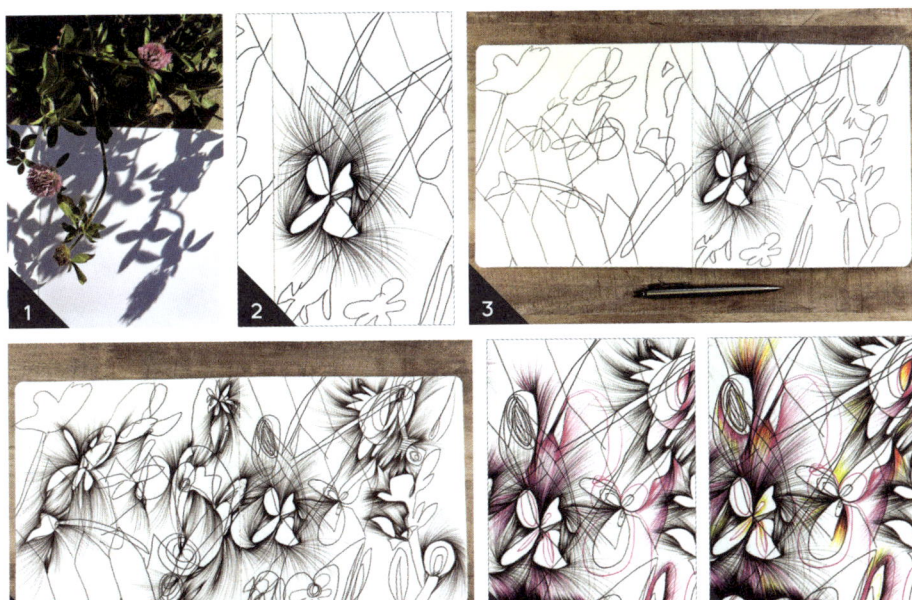

1. On a sunny day, head outside with your sketchbook and a pen. Document shadows that grab your attention by laying your sketchbook on the ground and tracing the shadows directly onto the page. Stop and trace different shadows, adding new shapes until you fill the page. Make these tracings as detailed or as loose as you like and include organic and geometric shapes for maximum interest.

2. Find an area in the drawing that grabs your attention and start there. Draw more lines and shapes or start shading straight away. Using the technique of your choice, shade inside or around the shapes that you find interesting.

3. Continue around the composition in this fashion, developing areas that you find interesting and obscuring unappealing areas by drawing over the top of them.

4. Once you've filled in some space all around the drawing, work on connecting these areas into one unified image. You might do that with shading, by drawing in more shapes, repeating an interesting shape that appears elsewhere, or adding in some pattern or mark-making.

5. This is a good point to add in another color. Work on top of the existing drawing and shade in new areas. Use it to emphasize your focal point. Add the color throughout the composition so that it looks purposeful.

6. Call it a day or add in a third color. As I used yellow, I mainly added it on top or near areas that were already shaded.

# ABSTRACT
## FROM PHOTOS

On my daily walks, I'm always on the lookout for interesting things that I find along the way. I take photos and collect them in a folder on my phone titled "Abstraction Inspiration." On those "no idea days" that happen from time to time, I can pull something from this folder as inspiration. In this project, I'll share my process for turning a photo into an abstract drawing.

### TOP TIP

Work large so that you have lots of room for experimentation and play. Try drawing in blind contour, looking only at the photo and not at the paper as you draw.

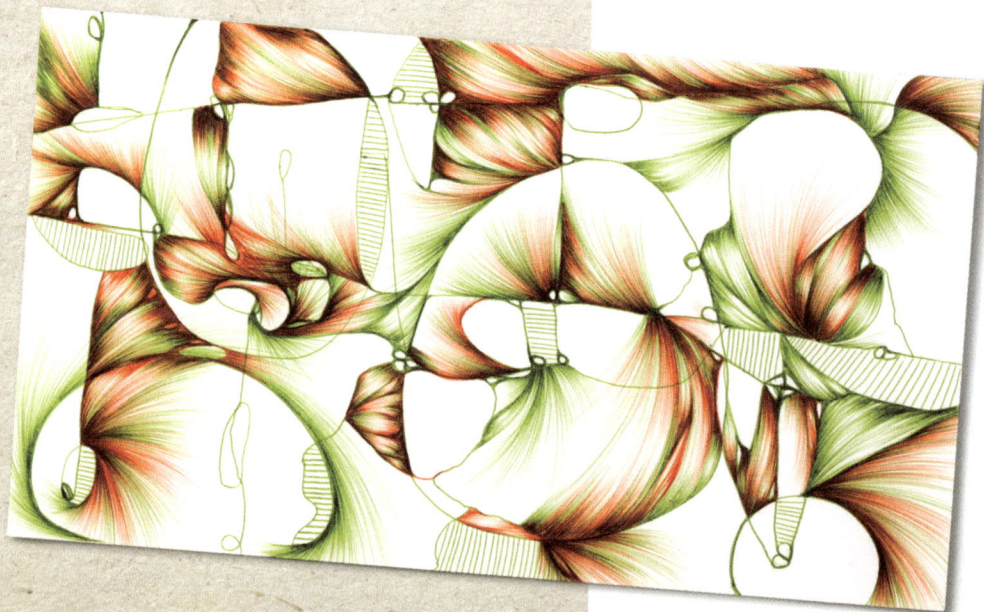

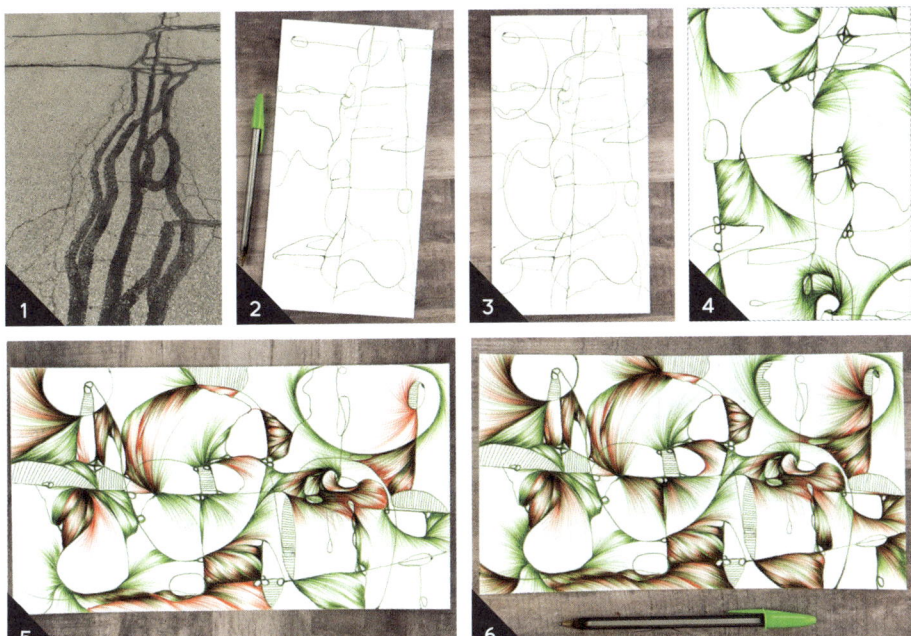

1. Take a walk anywhere you like. Look for patterns, textures, anything that catches your eye and take photos of them. Don't worry about how you're going to draw it, just collect images. Then choose a photo as inspiration and take some time to study it carefully. What attracts you to it? What parts of the photo do you want to include and which parts will you ignore?

2. With a pen of your choice, draw shapes that mimic what you see in the photo. Let this be as loose as you please, not concerning yourself with copying things exactly.

3. Repeat the process until you have broken up the space into both small and large shapes. Feel free to add your own shapes that aren't in the photo. Now put the photo away.

4. Using your lightest color first, begin to shade in and around shapes that you are attracted to. There are no rules to how or what you shade, just add value where you feel like it. You don't need to fill in the whole space, just make sure the negative spaces look purposeful.

5. If you get to a point where you don't know what to do next, choose a new color or a new shading technique. Another option is to add in some pattern, such as straight lines, to contrast with the organic forms.

6. Continue working until you've got a balance of negative and positive space and there is a flow around the composition. Also determine the orientation of the piece, as you may prefer it the opposite way up.

# FLORAL MANDALA

Floral elements have made an appearance in my art for as long as I can remember. Some come straight from my imagination, while others are based on real flowers. In this project, you'll work from life or from photos to build a vocabulary of floral-based abstractions that can be turned into a circular mandala design.

## YOU WILL NEED

- Sketchbook or smooth paper
- 10 x 10in (25.5 x 25.5cm) Bristol board
- Pens in three to five colors
- Pencil
- Eraser
- Ruler
- Markers or colored pencils (optional)

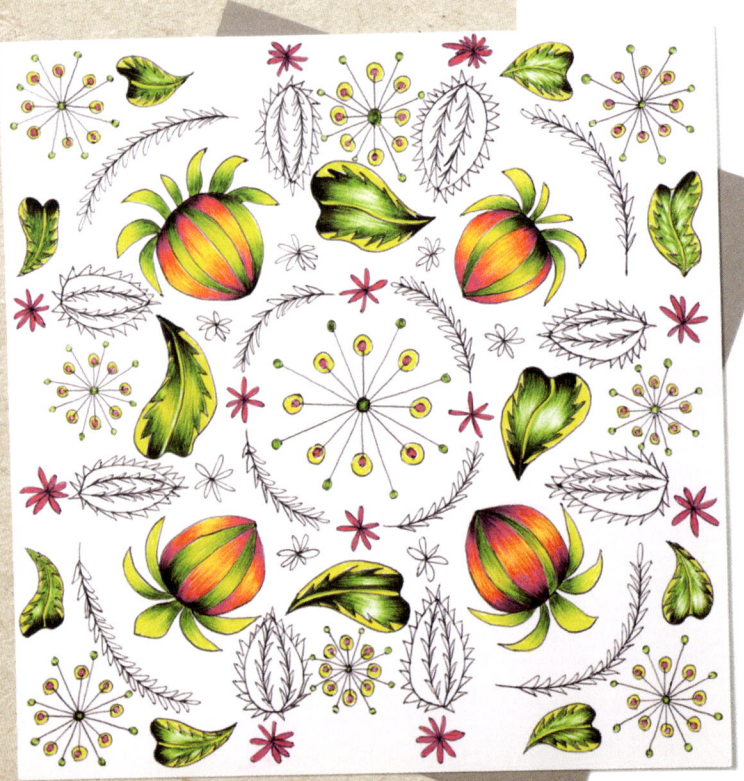

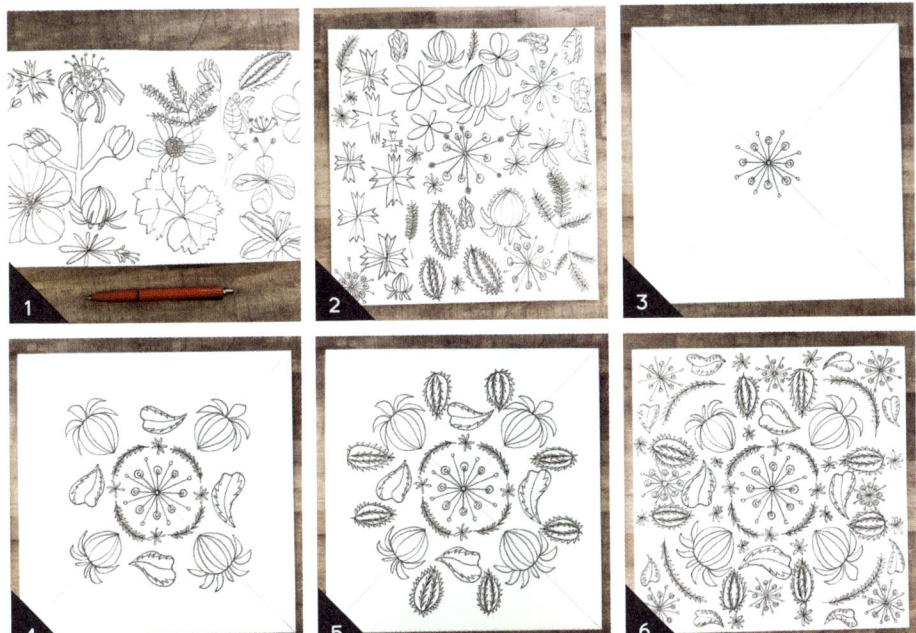

1. Fill a page in your sketchbook with flower and foliage drawings. Work from photos or from life. Challenge yourself to draw in pen, describing the shapes and textures of each flower with a minimum number of lines. Relax and don't concern yourself with the outcome. Just observe closely and draw what you see.

2. Choose some of your favorite drawings and draw them again, this time trying to simplify the shapes even further. Practice drawing each flower several times, refining as you go, until they start to come easily to you. Include a variety of different floral shapes.

3. Prepare the Bristol board by using a pencil and ruler to lightly draw two diagonal lines from corner to corner. Choose one of your floral shapes to draw (with pen) right in the center where the two lines intersect.

4. Circle the central flower with one or two contrasting flower forms.

5. Repeat the process, creating a third circle, with one or two new flowers.

6. To create some unity in your composition, start to repeat flower forms you've already drawn. Keep working in concentric circles until you've filled the page and erase the pencil guidelines. Leave it as is, or add some color with markers, pencils, or pen. Limit your color palette to three to five colors so that it doesn't become too busy.

# INSPIRATION GALLERY

To further inspire your ballpoint drawing journey, here is a selection of ballpoint illustrations I've made over the years.

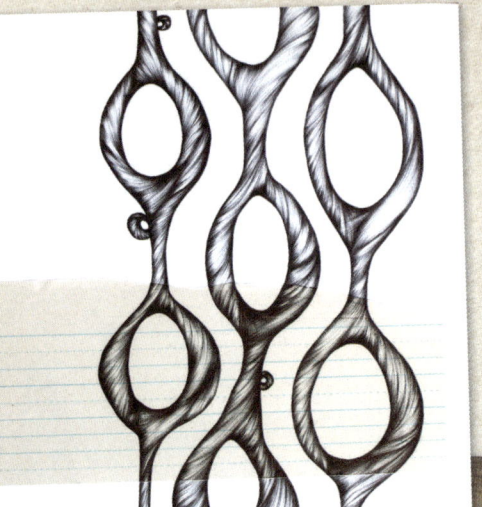

## FLOW THROUGH YOU

Collage paper and black ballpoint pen on cradled hardboard, 2015.

I've always been drawn to organic bone-like forms and the contrast of negative and positive spaces.

## JUST JACK

Collage paper, Prismacolor pencil, and black ballpoint pen on cradled hardboard, 2012.

A portrait of my stepson when he was 12 years old.

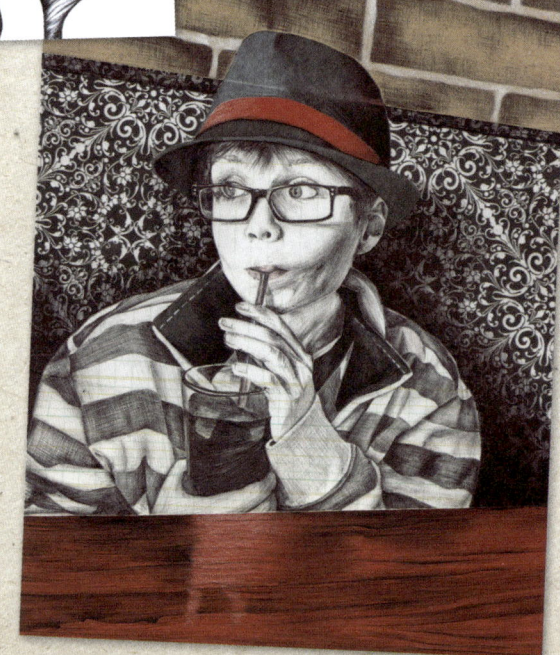

## TINKER'S ROOT WOOD CREATION

Collaged paper, black ballpoint pen and white Prismacolor pencil on cradled hardboard, 2012.

I was commissioned to create 10 original works for the Tinker Swiss Home Museum in Rockford, Illinois. This drawing features furniture that the homeowner, Robert Tinker, made himself. This beautiful table and chair set is all made of root wood, that was masterfully jigsawed together. It was a challenge to render all of the nooks and crannies of the wood.

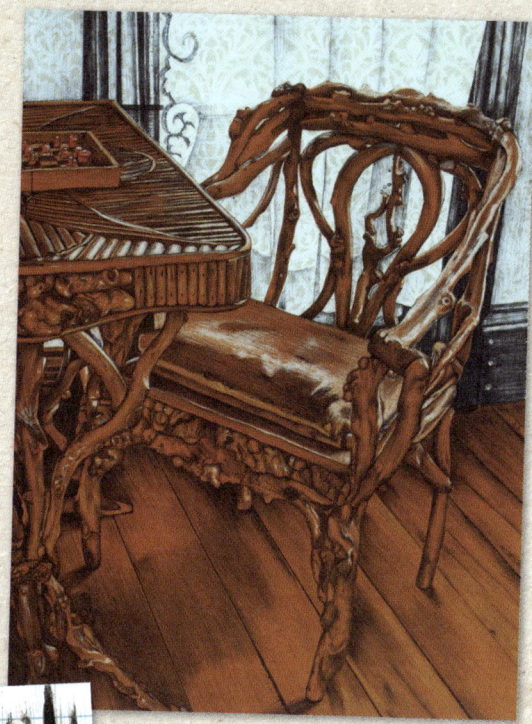

## RED-BELLIED WOODPECKER

Ballpoint pen and Prismacolor pencil on lined notepaper, 2014.

For many years, I drew birds of all kinds, often on lined notebooks or graph paper so that they were reminiscent of field drawings.

## ABOUT THE AUTHOR

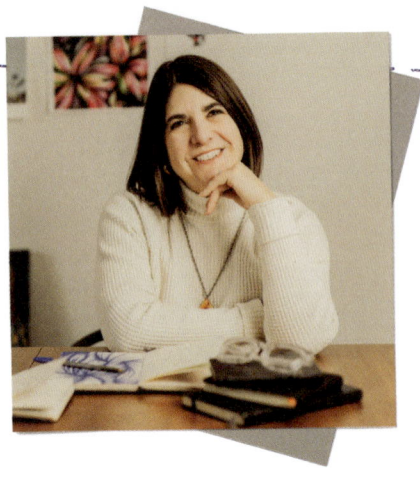

Jennifer Mullin is a mixed media artist and art instructor, who got serious about art in 2006, when the art she was making started cluttering her house.

In 2016, Jen's sketchbook drawings went viral on Pinterest. She was inundated with requests to learn her ballpoint techniques so she created the popular Jen + Ink online courses, enjoyed by students worldwide.

Besides being an artist, Jennifer is a project manager, daily walker, gardener, reader, cook, traveler, life-long Cubs fan, and lifter of heavy weights.

She lives in Madison, Wisconsin with her husband and their two cats, Cleo and Richard.

Find more about Jennifer's work at jennifer-mullin.com.

## ACKNOWLEDGMENTS

Thank you to my "LP" Chris Strawbridge, for being my biggest fan and dealing with me on Sunday nights when I was tired and hungry after a long weekend of book writing.

To my parents, John and Carla Mullin: please forgive me for missing every family gathering over the summer while I was writing this book. Thank you for supporting me in all of my artistic endeavors over the years.

To my brother, Kyle Mullin: thank you for checking in every Saturday and listening to me vent and worry about making my deadlines.

To Heather Smith and Becky Pelley for their pep talks, friendship, and art guidance during the process of writing this book.

To Lauren V. Davis and the Mastermind members: I might have given up on this project had it not been for your encouragement, support, and insights while I was writing this book. Thank you.

To Bryan Reichling and the SpeedPro team for your patience and understanding with me on Monday mornings when I showed up exhausted after writing all weekend.

Thank you to Clare Ashton for her superb editing and encouragement, and to my D&C team—Nigel Browning, Jess Cropper, and Lucy Ridley. Thank you for taking a chance on me and supporting me through the process of writing my first book.

And lastly, thank you to the Jen + Ink online community, without whom I wouldn't be writing this book today.

# INDEX

A catalogue record for this book is available from the British Library.

ISBN-13: 9781446315293 hardback
ISBN-13: 9781446315309 EPUB

This book has been printed on paper from approved suppliers and made from pulp from sustainable sources.

MIX
Paper | Supporting responsible forestry
FSC
www.fsc.org
FSC® C020056

Printed in China by Leo Paper Products Ltd for: David and Charles, Ltd Suite A, Tourism House, Pynes Hill, Exeter, EX2 5WS

10 9 8 7 6 5 4 3 2 1

**Publishing Director:** Ame Verso
**Senior Commissioning Editor:** Nigel Browning
**Publishing Manager:** Jeni Chown
**Editor:** Jessica Cropper
**Project Editor:** Clare Ashton
**Lead Designer:** Sam Staddon
**Designer:** Lucy Ridley
**Pre-press Designer:** Susan Reansbury
**Art Direction:** Tom Hargreaves
**Photography:**
Tom Hargreaves
Jennifer Mullin
Ember & Birch Photography (pages 4 and 5)
**Production Manager:** Beverley Richardson

David and Charles publishes high-quality books on a wide range of subjects. For more information visit **www.davidandcharles.com**.

Share your makes with us on social media using **#dandcbooks** and follow us on Facebook and Instagram by searching for **@dandcbooks**.

Layout of the digital edition of this book may vary depending on reader hardware and display settings.